Job seekers need a current, straightforward and realistic assessment of what to expect, along with helpful instruction to navigate what can be a difficult and frustrating process. Ken Murdock's most recent book delivers this guide to job seekers, including practical and real world examples of pitfalls to avoid, and methods to increase the success of each phase of the job search process. Wisdom of experience from a corporate leader and executive searcher is evident in this book, which will motivate the job seeker to persevere, while providing effective ways to make it through the maze that is the current job seeking environment.

James Brady
(Real Estate and Mortgage Executive)

Ken has described very well the mindset of recruiters and candidates alike in a competitive job market. With more candidates than ever applying for positions, the need to differentiate oneself as a viable candidate is critical. Ken's discussion of the tips, tricks, and pitfalls provides timely, pertinent information for job seekers.

Diane Harrington
HR Director (Manufacturing Company)

Your Complete Guide to
Job Search and Career Change

Your Complete Guide to Job Search and Career Change

Ken Murdock

Contents

Getting Started

The US Department of Labor tells us that the average person starting a job today will change careers three to five times in his or her working life. That is not just changing jobs, such as an accountant moving from one accounting firm to another. This statistic refers to a person who is a plumber changing to a sales rep, then to a psychologist, then to a school teacher, then to a retail shop owner, and retiring as a real estate investor.

As events happen in our lives, some of them of our own making and some a result of the outside environment, we are constantly exposed to new interests, changing circumstances, and opportunities. Any of these influences can lead to the desire or the necessity of changes in how we earn a living, where we live, and how we spend our time.

The days of our parents or grandparents who may have worked in a job for the same company for forty years and then retired with the gold watch are gone, and it is hard to imagine the circumstances that could ever bring them back. Because of advances in technology and communications, many of those jobs can be done in places where the wage rate is much lower than in the United States. Change in our lives is going to happen, so the only real choice we have is how we react to it. Fortunately, we are not helpless in dealing with these changes. I am not going to tell you that it is simple or easy to make a major change in your work life, but I will tell you that it does not have to be the laborious, anxious, and awkward experience that many perceive it to be at the outset.

How can I say that without even knowing you? Because human nature has not changed in thousands of years, and because I have worked with hundreds of people who have successfully made the transition. These people came from different levels of education, backgrounds, skill levels, experiences, wants, and needs. Some were forced to make a change due to company closures, downsizing, mergers, acquisitions, or because the company decided to "go in a different direction." Others saw opportunities in new fields and decided that they wanted to try something different.

While they were as different as can be in many areas, there are a few qualities that virtually all my clients had in common. Probably most important was that they had transferable skills and personality traits that are useful in any endeavor. I am not referring to specific, technical skills such as how to repair an electric circuit. I am talking about skills and qualities that everyone picks up in varying amounts just by showing up for work every day...human relations skills, organization skills, the capacity to learn, perseverance, patience, curiosity...skills that, when they are applied to a new path can create value for an employer or for the individual who may want to go out on his or her own.

My point is that you know more than you think or realize that you know, and you can do more than you may realize that you can do. You are stuck where you are, whether you are employed or not, only if you think you are stuck there. That is not a Pollyanna, feel good, pep talk phrase. That is a fact. I know because I have seen hundreds of people successfully make the transition from one position to another by following the guidelines that I am going to share with you in this book.

You may be asking yourself what makes me qualified to tell you how to adapt to a change that was forced on you or how to make the change that you know you want to make in your job or career. Good question, and I will do my best to answer it.

First, I have owned and operated a successful executive recruiting company for the last decade. I started it in January of 2000, and it is been not only a great business for me but also a tremendous learning experience. It has been in my recruiting business that I have met and worked with the people and the organizations that have taught me a large part of what I am going to share with you.

When people ask me what I do, I sometimes jokingly tell them that I run an industrial dating service. That is really what the recruiting industry is at its core. Think of it as similar to the online matchmaking services that people use to find their true love these days. These services provide a mechanism for people to meet each other. People are busy in their careers and for the most part, they need a way to increase the numbers of other people they meet and also to increase the probability that the people whom they do meet are compatible with them. Each person fills out a profile that tells others about them, such as their interests, hobbies, and ambitions. Each member of the service can look at these profiles and determine whether they would like to meet the other person. If both parties agree, they get together and see if there is a good match.

The recruiting industry is similar to the matchmaking industry. Two parties - a company and an individual - fill out profiles that we call job descriptions and resumes. Each party reviews the profile of the other and decides whether they want to get together and discuss an alliance where they work together. If it works out, the individual gets a job, the company gets a new employee, and the recruiter gets paid.

It is that "getting paid" part that taught me some very valuable lessons that I will share with you in the first chapter.

The other factor that has provided me a valuable blend of skills for helping others to make job and career changes is my other profession. I teach Marketing in the School of Business at a major state university, and I am an adjunct professor of business at another private university. Marketing is all about the processes of making a product or service desirable in the eyes of the consumer. In the employment game, that consumer is the hiring company. The mix between recruiting and teaching Marketing is an ideal one for me because what I have learned in each position has helped me immensely in the other.

Here is my definition of Marketing: "The process of creating the perception of value and the desire to acquire a product or service." In the process of changing jobs or careers, you are the product, and the mission is to create the perception of your value and the desire to acquire you as an employee for the firm.

By combining what I have learned from my client companies as a recruiter and in my marketing studies and practice, I have found that a great deal of what most conventional wisdom says about how to proceed on a job and/or career hunt is just plain wrong. Some of it is ineffective and some of it is actually detrimental to the job seeker.

I am going to show you how to market yourself in such a way that you will:

- greatly enhance your chances of getting an interview,

- know how to prepare for the interview,

- learn what to do after the interview, and,

- know how to negotiate the best deal you can get when the company makes you an offer of employment.

Whatever your background, experience, level of education or current state of employment, you can give yourself a competitive advantage by approaching the change with a new mindset and some tools you may not have not had in the past.

Understand that whether you do not have a job or you have one and want to make a change, the first step is to get someone to notice you. Someone has to say to themselves, "This person looks interesting...I think I would like to talk to him/her." Until that happens, nothing else that you do matters, not even a little bit. This is where most people get bogged down in following the rules and making themselves look like everyone else, which is exactly what you do not want to do.

Ask yourself this question: "What has conventional thinking done for me so far?" The answer is probably that it has not done for you what you want, or else you would not be reading this book! Are you ready to step outside of conventional thinking and bend a few "rules" in the job search? Are you ready to get serious and try something new? Can you imagine opening yourself up to the possibility of really energizing your job search? If so, read on...

Chapter 1:

"Let Me Introduce Myself": The Cover Letter

The whole purpose of a cover letter is to get someone to read your resume, develop interest in talking to you, and invite you to come in for an interview. That is it. There is no other purpose. The cover letter is not an autobiography, an editorial treatise, or an excuse for stylistic showmanship. It should be short, to the point, and focus on introducing the writer and the resume that accompanies the letter.

However, none of this means that the cover letter has to be boring or "plain vanilla". In fact, if you can write it in such a way that it sets you apart from the crowd in positive way, it is all the better. There are lots of types of cover letters, which we will explore shortly, but there are a few basic guidelines that all of them share.

First, they are short, three to four paragraphs at most, and no more than one page. You know why you are writing the letter and the reader knows why you are writing the letter, so there is no point in taking a long time to get to the point of the letter. So, use the first paragraph to state what both of you already know. You are either applying for a position that you know about or you are announcing your interest in working for the organization and asking them to consider you as a candidate for some unstated position. In either circumstance, you have a choice of presenting yourself as just another plain vanilla job seeker or as someone who stands out from the crowd.

Here is the difference. The plain vanilla job seeker says something like this: "I am very interested in the marketing associate position that I saw described in your advertisement in _____ trade journal." Someone who intends to stand out from the crowd would get the same point across, but do it in a much more compelling manner: "The advertisement that you placed in the _____ trade journal for a marketing associate sounds like it was written just for me. I think I am the perfect candidate for this position."

The second paragraph and the third (if necessary) are where you sell yourself to the reader. Tell why you are uniquely qualified for the position by citing your experience, any specific skills you possess, your interest in the type of work, and an example of what you have done in the past that qualifies you for the job. The objective is to get the reader to understand what you already know...that you are writing this letter specifically because of your interest in this particular job. It is not a form letter that you send out to everyone with only one or two minor changes for each position.

Your final paragraph states that your resume is attached and that you would appreciate the reader reviewing it. Ask for a meeting to discuss how you and the company may be a great match for each other. Thank the reader for considering your interest and qualifications for the job, and state that you will look forward to hearing from him or her about a meeting. Then close the letter.

That is the format for a letter in which you do not know them and they do not know you. It is straightforward, with a little flair of creativity to get the reader's attention. It is a pretty "safe" format that does not go overboard or make you sound desperate. I know that this format works because I used it myself many years ago to get a job interview. The hiring manager specifically told me that he liked the way I came across in the letter and that it prompted him to invite me in for an interview. I contacted this company without knowing whether there was a particular position available or not. I just wanted to let them know who I was and that I had an interest in working there.

There is a lesson in this experience. That is, do not limit yourself just to companies that are advertising to fill positions. Most companies, as I have seen firsthand, do not publicize or advertise that they are trying to fill a position. The main reason is that they do not want to be inundated with unqualified candidates sending in their resumes. It takes an incredible amount of time to sort through letters and resumes, and most of them are not worth the time it takes to read them. That is time that most people running a business do not have. Instead, they either "put the word out" to current employees or to others who might know a good candidate, or they hire a recruiter to do the sorting and the sifting and then bring them the best of what they can find.

If you can write a good letter and get yourself noticed by someone in the company who can make a decision, you may be very attractive to that company. There are two reasons. One is that you may be a great candidate who can solve their problem of needing someone. The other is that if they hire you directly, they save a lot of money that they do not have to pay someone like me, a recruiter. Recruiters' fees often run as high as thirty five percent of the first year's income for the person hired. Those fees are paid by the hiring company. Recruiters have to charge these fees to cover their costs of finding people and for all the "dry holes" they drill where they put in substantial time, effort, and expense to find people, and the job "dies" before it is filled. If they can hire you without paying some else for the finding you, you are saving them a lot of money.

One guiding principle I have always advised candidates to remember is that a cover letter ought to be authentic. By that I mean that it ought to give the reader an accurate representation of who you really are and how you think. If you are a person who is low-key, reserved, and you operate without a lot of flair in your life, it may be beneficial to liven up your resume a little, but not so much that you come across as an entirely different person than you really are. Avoid the old "bait and switch" tactic that some unscrupulous retailers have used, where they advertise a product on sale, but when you get to the store to buy it, they are out of stock and try to convince you to buy something else, usually a more expensive substitute. You should not try to portray yourself as someone that you really are not. It will come out sooner or later anyway, so there is no point in trying to deceive anyone.

However, if you are one who likes to try the unusual, who does not mind going down the less traveled highway, there is another option for cover letters that might appeal to you. This type of cover letter can be used in any situation, but it is ideal for those jobs that have a lot of candidates vying for interviews. It is also ideal if you do not know the recipient and do not know anyone else who knows the recipient either. This is where a little understanding of human nature comes into play.

One constant in human relations is that most people rarely do anything for anyone else unless it is in their own best interests to do so. In other words, it is unlikely that someone is going to do anything to help you unless helping you also brings benefit to them in some way. Maybe the benefit to them is that they will feel good about themselves for doing something for someone else. People use that as a basis for charitable giving all the time. Maybe they think that if they do something good for someone else, the favor will be returned to them in some way in the future. The benefit to the giver may not be apparent on the surface and they may not even know it themselves, but there is something that motivates them to help others or they would not do it. If you understand this, you can use it to your advantage.

Most cover letters to people that the writer does not know follow a conventional format that says something like this:

Dear Sir/Madam,

I am interested in a career in sales/marketing/accounting (whatever). Your firm is one that fits my criterion of an industry leader. I believe I could be a valuable asset to your company, and would appreciate the opportunity to speak to you about how my skills and experience may be a good fit for your organization.

My resume is attached for your review. I can be available for an interview at your convenience. Please let me know a good time for us to meet. I hope to hear from you and meet you soon.

Sincerely,
John/Jane Doe

Sound familiar? Have you sent out a cover letter and resume with something like that to introduce yourself? Probably, yes. Have you heard back from anyone? Maybe, but probably not. The reason is that hiring managers get letters like this from people they do not know all the time, and yours is just another one on the pile. If you feel like staying with convention and playing it "safe" with your cover letter, ask yourself how that has worked for you so far. If you are honest with yourself, the answer is pretty simple. It has not worked very well at all. If you have not been invited to an interview with the "safe" method, what do you have to lose by trying something new? There is a very important principle to understand here. That is, it takes only one successful effort to get the interview you want. If you get more than that, great, but realize that it is better to get someone's attention and secure one interview than to lump yourself with everyone else and hope that your resume is drawn out of the pile. In my experience with candidates, those who have been willing to defy conventional thinking in the job search process have been more successful in getting interviews and job offers than those who follow the old, standard procedures.

In the marketing profession, there is a concept called "cause" marketing. It refers to a type of marketing involving the cooperative efforts of a "for profit" business and a non-profit organization for mutual benefit. An example might be an advertising campaign in which a restaurant says that for every dessert they sell, they will donate one dollar to a particular charity. People who might not otherwise order dessert may do so with the excuse that they are helping the non-profit organization. Most people are willing to go out of their way to help worthy causes if it is easy to do it.

So, consider for a moment how you might use cause marketing in your job search to make you stand out from the crowd. Keep in mind the existing set of circumstances. You do not know the recipient. You may not even know anything about them, such as whether the recipient is a man or a woman, their age, or anything else. The recipient does not know you either, and has no incentive to help you unless they perceive benefit to themselves or to their organization by doing so. You are competing with dozens, maybe hundreds of others who want the same thing you want, which is for the recipient to review your resume and invite you in for an interview.

It is time to get creative and think outside of the normal boundaries of conventional wisdom. Here is where cause marketing can be useful in your job search.

Every community has well-known charitable organizations, such as food pantries, Boys and Girls Clubs, animal shelters, or the Red Cross. All of them need volunteer help on a regular basis. Just about everyone, at least in theory if not financially, either supports these organizations or is favorable toward their existence and their mission. The best deals are those where everyone comes out a winner, and this is an opportunity for you to make that happen. Consider a cover letter that uses cause marketing in such a way that you, the interviewer, and the charitable organization all come out feeling good about the experience. A letter might say something like this:

Dear Mr./Ms Jones,

The position you have advertised for an environmental engineer seems tailor made for me. Your company is a well-known leader in this arena, and may be a great match for the skills and talents I can offer in this field. The projects I have worked on and the experience I can bring to this position would enable me to contribute immediately as a member of your team. Because your company is known as a leader in the field and is at the top of a lot of job seekers' lists for career opportunities, I am sure that you receive quite a few resumes and requests for interviews.

Obviously, that is what I seek as well, but I am willing to offer a unique incentive for the opportunity to visit with you about my interest in your company. I have selected three local charitable organizations that I believe make our community a better place to live. Each of these charitable organizations needs volunteer help to accomplish their mission. The charities I have selected are the local food bank, the animal shelter, and the Meals on Wheels program for senior citizens.

In return for the opportunity to visit with you about career opportunities with your company, I will volunteer four hours at the charity you choose. The charity will get the free labor, you will have the satisfaction of knowing that you had a part in helping them in their mission, and I will get an interview. Everyone wins. I will send you written confirmation of the time I spend in my volunteer efforts.

Please consider this as a genuine indicator of my interest in your company. I can be available at your convenience. I hope to hear from you and meet you soon.

Sincerely,
John/Jane Doe

Remember, the whole idea is to set yourself apart from the crowd. You want to do that in such a way that you come across as respectful, professional, genuine, and interested in the organization. This type of letter covers all those qualities. You also demonstrate creativity with such a novel approach. You are not offering a bribe or anything that smacks of any direct, tangible favor to the reader. It is a "feel good" opportunity for everyone. Pick any charities that you know have universal appeal. The reader cannot help but admire your genuine interest in gaining an interview, and may want to talk to you just because you demonstrated such a unique approach to setting up a meeting between you and him or her. There is also a very strong probability that the reader will consider that you can bring the same creativity and perseverance to the job, which will make you even more attractive in their eyes.

The key element here is that you have to actually perform the volunteer service. Failure to perform as you said you would will put you in a worse situation than if you had never made the offer in the first place, and the reader may very well want to see that you have performed the service before you get the interview.

If you knew for certain that you could get the interview you want in return for four hours of volunteer effort, would you do it? Of course you would! Certainly there is no guarantee that this tactic will get you an interview, but it will certainly improve your chances and get the reader's attention, and that is the first step in getting your resume read by someone who can make the interview happen.

So, what is the downside to this approach? I do not see one. Here is why:

1. The worst that could happen is that you do not get the interview. You already do not have the interview, so nothing has changed and you have lost nothing.

2. It is different than the traditional approach to cover letters and seeking interviews. So what? What has conventional thinking done for you so far? Remember, setting yourself apart from the crowd is the whole idea.

3. Think about this. Any company or individual who would be offended by such an approach is a strong signal that you may not want to work at a place like that anyway.

4. Assuming that you choose three charities for whom you will volunteer, the most number of hours of your time that it will cost you is twelve hours. If several companies choose the same charity, the same four hours of your volunteer efforts can satisfy each of them. Whether you choose three charities, or two, or four really is not important. What is important is that you have demonstrated an unusual degree of creativity and willingness to earn the interview with this type of effort.

This is just one suggestion as an alternative technique for getting an interview. With a little effort, you can probably come up with others that separate you from the crowd as effectively as this one does.

We have looked at letters that are mainly designed for people you do not know where you are trying to get a foot in the door with a complete stranger. The main idea is that you want to get someone to review your resume and invite you for a face-to-face interview, and the examples that we have seen so far can help you do that. Without question, however, the best letters are usually those that mention a mutual friend or contact. Most people are glad to offer assistance in this area, mainly because many of them have benefitted from "knowing someone" themselves.

The type of cover letter that works best depends on the relationship, if any, that the writer has with the addressee. If you know the person to whom the letter is directed, the letter can have a more familiar tone than if there is no relationship at all. Keep in mind that if you know the person very well, the letter can be much more personal and direct than if the relationship is a casual one. If the person to whom the letter is written is someone that you met recently or that you have known only on a casual basis, a letter that reminds them who you are and then asks them to review your resume is in order. This type of letter will go something like this:

Dear Mr./Ms Jones,

I am interested in making a career change, and I would appreciate your help as I explore new opportunities. When you and I worked together on the fund raising drive for the local community center I became interested in your organization as I learned more about it. I believe that my skills and experience in project management might be a good fit within your company.

My resume is attached for your review. I would appreciate the opportunity to visit with you in person about how XYZ company and I might be an ideal match for each other. If you can let me know a good time for a meeting that fits your schedule, I will make myself available at your convenience. I hope to hear from you and meet you soon.

Sincerely,
John/Jane Doe

The format for this type of letter is simple. Tell the reader why you are contacting them, remind them of how you know each other, and ask for a meeting.

Without question, the most effective cover letters are those that mention a mutual friend or acquaintance...a referral letter. If you have a friend who knows someone else well enough to recommend you to them, the chances are very good that the person to whom you have been recommended will respond positively to your request for him or her to review your resume and invite you in for an interview. It is all part of networking, and you should use it whenever you can. The format is simple and direct. Tell the reader that you have a mutual friend who recommended that you contact him or her, then ask for a meeting. It is a get-to-the-point type of letter. It should still be courteous and professional, but the main justification for asking the reader to review your resume and to invite you in for an interview is to comply with the unwritten rule of granting a favor for a friend. You know it and the reader knows it, so state your case and ask the reader to grant the request. Like other types of cover letters, it is short and direct:

Dear Mr./Ms Jones,

My friend Sarah Williams suggested that I contact you. Sarah mentioned that you and she were friends in college and that you would be a great contact for me to make in my efforts to make a career change. As an experienced sales manager, I am very interested in applying my skills and knowledge to the benefit of a leading company in the technology arena, and your company is one that certainly fits that criteria.

My resume is attached for your review. I would appreciate the opportunity to visit with you in person about how XYZ company and I might be an ideal match for each other. If you can let me know a good time for a meeting that fits your schedule, I will make myself available at your convenience. I hope to hear from you and meet you soon.

Sincerely,
John/Jane Doe

Chapter 2

The Importance of Your Resume

It was in April of my first year in the recruiting industry. I had made a few small placements, collected a few mid-level fees, and was actively working on my first big search for a new client. "Big" at that time was a fee in excess of twenty thousand dollars. I had met with the client to get a good idea of exactly what they wanted, and I was clear about the type of candidate they wanted to consider for their Chief Financial Officer position. This was an important position for them and they wanted to be very deliberate and demanding in the candidates they were willing to consider.

Over a period of a few weeks I had found three candidates whom I thought were technically qualified and had excellent experience, and I was very confident that my client would be very pleased with any of them. I had spoken with each candidate at length about the job, the company, the management, and the compensation. Each candidate was interested in discussing the position, so I proceeded to send their resumes to the client for consideration. My expectation was that the client would call me back to schedule three interviews.

To my great surprise and dismay, the client did call back, but to tell me that they did not like any of the resumes and would pass on all three candidates. They told me that none of the resumes seem to be a "fit" for them. When I asked more pointed questions about what exactly they meant by that, they told me that this position was a critical one for their company and that they were looking for more than skill sets to fill it. They wanted to talk to candidates who were as focused on a great fit as they were, and none of the resumes they had seen indicated anything at all about the people behind the skill sets and experience listed on the resume.

That is when it hit me, that companies (which are made up of people), want to hire people who fit with their culture, their way of doing things. There are lots of candidates who have outstanding skill sets and good experience, but companies want to talk to people that they believe have the same values, priorities, and the all-important people skills that make them a good fit with those who are already a part of the organization.

When the light came on, I began to ask myself how I could have been so naive in my first few placements. What it boiled down to was that I got lucky (a little bit), but there was a difference in the size and scope of the jobs as well. That is when I began to realize a very important fact about the recruiting industry. That is, *the higher the position, the more importance companies place on the person in addition to the skills and experience.* It is not that companies do not care about the type of person in lower level positions, but in the manufacturing trades (my recruiting specialty), there seems to be more of a focus on skills for the task in the hourly jobs and not so much concern with the people skills. However, as the responsibilities increase and there is more person-to-person interaction and less person-to-machine interaction, the focus is on both the skills *and* the person. That same logic is common in other industries as well. The more a person's job involves working with other people, the more emphasis companies place on the character and human relations skills of the candidate. *And that is precisely what most people ignore when they are constructing their resumes.*

The process that most candidates follow is generally some variation of the name, objective, experience, education, and references format. They use this format because they have been taught that this is the way it has always been done. They are convinced that most resumes are in the same format, and they do not want to break the rules by doing anything differently.

When I ask candidates how they came up with their resume, many of them tell me that they got a copy of someone else's resume and just put their own information into the same format, or they downloaded a resume template from somewhere on the Internet and just filled in the blanks with their own information.

Many also go outside for help and pay someone else to construct a beautiful resume for them. There is nothing wrong with that if the writer knows how to focus on the right information, but if all they are doing is making your own information look prettier on the page, it is a waste of money.

Either way they do it, many candidates take the attitude that they do not need to worry too much about the resume because once they get in front of the interviewer, they will impress them with their personalities and mastery of the subject. There is one big problem with this line of reasoning: *it is the resume that will, in large part, determine whether you get the interview in the first place.*

A resume has only one purpose...not two, not three, not five or six...just one. That purpose is to get you an interview! It does not matter how good you are at what you do, and it does not matter how wonderful your personality is, or how well you work and play with others. If you never get the chance to meet the person who makes the hiring decision, nothing else matters.

Because the resume is such a critical document, it is very important to avoid mistakes in it that will get it thrown out due to careless errors. One of the most glaring and inexcusable errors is the spelling error. Nothing will get your resume tossed more quickly than for the reader to see a misspelled word. There are several reasons, and it takes only one of them to eliminate you from consideration:

1. In this document that is supposed to create the first impression that the reader will have of you, you did not take the time to make it perfect. It makes you look like you do not care.

2. The reader thinks that if you are careless in this document, you would probably be the same way in your work for the company.

3. It makes you appear lazy, because using the spell check feature on today's word processing programs is so easy that there is no justification for not using it.

However, do not get too comfortable even if you do use the spell check feature on your word processor. There are some errors that word processors often do not find, such as the wrong form of a word. Examples are "two, too, to", "there, their, they are", and "your and you're". I have also seen many resumes in which the writer uses "lose" instead of "loose" (and vice versa) and "effect" where "affect" is the correct word (and vice versa). Confusing nouns with adjectives makes your skills in written communications appear to be lacking and spells trouble for a resume. Make sure that yours does not contain these errors.

No matter how well you follow all the grammatical, spelling, and content guidelines, there is still one more major stumbling block for most candidates in building their resumes. I have no idea where it came from or how it got started, but in my experience it is a "rule" that should be discarded and never brought up again. I am speaking of the "rule" that a resume has to be one page in length.

Bologna, or baloney...whichever! I have sent thousands of resumes to hiring managers, and I have never had the experience of one of those managers telling me that they did not like the resume because it was more than one page. Consider for a moment that you want to buy a new car, and you are very open to considering a variety of cars. So, you spend some time looking at various makes and models, and finally you narrow it down to four or five cars from which you will pick the one you buy. They are all made by different companies, so you go to each showroom and ask the sales counselor to show you the cars and to give you some information that you can take with you to review before you make the final decision. The first sales counselor gives you a one page sheet that has some information about one of the cars that you are considering. Then the sales counselor says, "There is a lot more you need to know about this car in order to make the right decision, but I could not make it fit on one page." You would think that this sales counselor has missed the whole point! You want to know as much as you can about the car, but instead of creating a multi-page information and promotional document, they've told you that their main objective was to fit what they could onto one page of paper.

The same logic applies to your resume. Certainly there is no need for endless, irrelevant information, but the whole idea of the resume is give the reader a good reason to want to meet you in person. If you make the first page good enough, the reader will want to read the rest of it. The challenge is in making the first page catch the attention of the reader in such a way that he or she wants to know more about you that is described on the next page or pages. That format is what will separate you from the crowd rather than blend into it.

Most resumes follow a format that goes something like this:

- Name and contact information

- Objective/Career Summary

- Work experience

- Education

- Referrals

There is nothing wrong with the order of those elements. Where most resumes fall short is in the content of each of those elements. Most resumes focus on a chronological job history, tell very little about you as a person, and are generally boring, no matter how you try to spruce them up with fancy fonts and five-dollar words. One of the main problems with this model is that it leaves it to the reader to try and figure out how you can bring benefit to them and their company, which is the whole idea behind hiring someone in the first place! People do not buy, and managers do not hire based on *features*, or facts about you. They hire based on *how* those facts will bring *benefits* to them, so your job is to point out those benefits.

Let's go back to car example mentioned earlier. If you were to into the showroom to look at a particular car, the sales counselor might point out to you that the car you are considering has a three hundred twenty seven cubic inch, V-8 engine. That is a feature, or a fact about the car. However if the sales counselor then says, "This car has enough power to get you onto the highway from the acceleration lane without getting run over by a big truck," that is a benefit, and as I mentioned earlier, people buy (and hire) based on benefits, not features. Most resumes are feature-heavy and benefit-light, when they should actually be equally balanced. If you give them only half the story (the features), you are not providing them with the reasons why they ought to talk to you in person, and that makes you look just like everyone else.

You may be one of the most talented, creative, hard-working people on the hemisphere, but how is the reader supposed to know these things about you? There is a simple answer. You tell them! This is where most resumes are lacking. They say nothing about the qualities of the person that may be attractive to the reader. If the resume simply reveals the positions you have had and where you have worked, the reader has no way of knowing anything at all about your qualities that separate you from the crowd. So, you have to put something on the first page (the "get their attention" page) that helps them see benefits to having you in their organization and makes them want to read the rest of the document.

This is also where most people get a little hesitant and cautious because they do not want to come across as too self-important or bragging. They are reluctant to "blow their own horn," so to speak. The point to remember here is that the resume provides a degree of separation from you, the person. It is almost as if another person was telling about the skills and abilities you can bring to the job. So, do not hesitate to come right out and say that you are creative, or persevering, or well organized, or that you have great "people" skills, or a whole host of other desirable qualities. This reluctance can only hurt your chances of getting the interview. Think of it this way...the resume is supposed to give the reader an accurate description of you, the candidate. If you have qualities that you know would be desirable and valuable to the organization where you want to work, you are holding back and not giving them a complete description if you do not give them the information that will help them make the right choice.

Now that we have covered the essential elements of the resume, let's put the format together.

Your Contact Information

The first element to any resume should be your name and contact information that includes your phone number, address, and e-mail address. All of this information should be centered at the top of the page.

Two warnings about your e-mail accounts are appropriate here. First, do not use an e-mail that is sexually suggestive or indicative of irresponsible behavior. I have seen e-mail addresses on resumes such as "hotforladies@(provider).com and "rocksnosalt@(provider).com. If you want to use something like that just for personal communications between you and your friends, go ahead, but it will cost you if you put something like that on a resume. It does not look professional, and it is so easy to avoid that problem by having a non-suggestive e-mail address.

The other warning is to avoid joint e-mail accounts on your contact information. If you and your special someone (spouse, significant other) want to share an e-mail such as "tomandsusan@(provider).com" for communications with your friends, you are certainly free to do so. However, get your own e-mail address to list on your contact information on your resume or to put on a job application. Recruiters and hiring authorities want to feel that they are dealing directly and exclusively with a candidate rather than with a committee, and an individual e-mail account promotes that assumption.

The same caveats extend to your phone greeting. Your contact information on your resume should have your phone number included. That number should be the one that the reader can call with a reasonable expectation of reaching you. If your automated greeting is inappropriate, you may be sabotaging your efforts to get an interview. A few years ago I was considering a young man for a sales position with a valued client. I had spoken with the young man on the phone a couple of times, once when he called me and again when I called him and he answered. On the third time that I needed to talk to him, I called his phone number and heard his voice mail greeting when he did not answer. The greeting was a simple rhyme, "You called my phone, but I ain't here...I just went out to get a beer." The job was one that would have paid about twelve thousand dollars more annually than what he was earning at the time, and included a company car that would have been worth an additional twelve to fourteen thousand dollars per year when the use of the car, the maintenance on it, the fuel, and insurance was considered. With the realization that my client judges me on the quality of the candidates I send to them, I was not about to send this person in for an interview, especially for a job that involved driving a company car. His phone greeting may have created a few chuckles among his friends but it cost him at least twenty five thousand dollars in a missed opportunity.

Objective/Career Summary

The next element of the resume is your Objective Statement OR your Career Summary. If you are in the early stages of your career and do not have a lot of experience yet, the objective statement is preferred for two reasons. First, it allows you to state specifically what you want to do, and by doing so you appear as someone who has a clearly focused career intention. Second, you do not yet have a career to summarize, so the career summary is not yet appropriate for you. Use the objective statement if you are seeking your first "real" job, or even your second one if your first job has clearly been an experience that you want to put behind you and start fresh.

We will deal with the objective statement first. Your first order of business is to be specific. A vague, rambling, "cover all the bases" objective statement will get your resume tossed out before anyone takes the time to read the rest of it. Recruiters and hiring managers alike will give you about four to five seconds to get their attention with your resume, and the first part of it that they look at is your objective statement.

A non-specific objective statement might read something like this: "A position with a leading organization that will allow me to use my skills and education for the benefit of the company and myself." A statement like that says nothing about the industry, the position, or even the general type of work that this person wants to do.

You should have a specific objective statement for each position you want to pursue. A specific statement helps the reader understand what you have to offer as well as what you are looking for in your job or career search. Not only is it preferable, it is essential. There are two reasons:

1. You do not want to leave it up to the reader to try to figure out what you want to do. If you cannot tell them what job you want, they are not going to take the time to figure it out for you. By stating clearly what job you are seeking, you are not eliminating yourself from consideration for other opportunities. Even if they do not have the specific job that is a one hundred percent match for your aspirations, they may well put you in contention for one that is eighty percent what you specify and maybe twenty percent of responsibilities and challenges that you had not considered.

2. By being specific in your objective, you are letting the reader know that you are a person who has a plan and a goal. It makes you look more focused, directed, and purposeful, and those are all good qualities that employers admire and like to see in candidates.

Here are a few examples of specific objective statements:

1. "A position as a budget analyst for a leading company in the defense industry."

2. "A position as a sales representative in the pharmaceutical industry."

3. "A position as an operations manager for a leading metal fabrication operation."

On several searches I have done for sales rep positions in the various industries, I have contacted candidates who sounded great on the phone and indicated real interest in the position. I would always ask them to send their resumes to me as an e-mail attachment so that I could review it before sending it to the client company. Then, when I would get the resume, having already explained the job and the requirements to them in great detail, I would see a sentence at the top of the page that said "Seeking a position in medical equipment sales" or some other position that had nothing to do with the job I discussed with them.

Obviously, these candidates were immediately eliminated from consideration. In your haste to send your resume to a recruiter or an employer, be sure to check that you do not make the mistake of having an objective statement that fits a different job.

The Career Summary

The Career Summary should be a short, concise (1 - 3 sentences) statement that defines you as a professional and compels the hiring manager to keep reading. This summary should make it clear what you want to do without coming right out and making an objective statement. For example, you might say:

- "Award winning, quota-busting sales professional with proven success in the B2B CRM software market.

- Ten year record of achieving minimum of 15% growth in numbers of accounts and retaining existing business.

- Consistently ranked first or second in nation-wide sales numbers in a sales force of 45 representatives.

By having a summary like this one, you have made it very clear that you are a great sales person and that a top sales position is your objective. The key is to write the summary in such a way that the reader can see what you have achieved and what you are targeting in a new position.

If you have had other positions in your career that have nothing to do with what you want to do in a new job, do not mention them in the summary. The summary should be focused on leading the reader to a logical conclusion of what you want to do. A disparate list of accomplishments that are unrelated to your target job will only confuse the reader.

With resumes in general and in career summaries in particular, you get some poetic license to write with incomplete sentences, so avoid using "I" statements. You do not need to write your autobiography or refer to anything that does not pertain to the position you seek. This is where it is not only OK, but advisable to use strong, action verbs and terminology unique to the industry. By doing so, you offer a almost visual image to the reader of what you have done and can do for them.

Chapter 3

Describe Yourself Effectively

This is where we begin a significant departure from the typical, generic resume. You have just written either your objective statement or your career summary. If you used the career summary, you have told the reader something about your professional accomplishments. Remember my earlier comments about how companies want to hire people that they believe will fit well in their culture and who have the values, priorities, and interests that they want in the person they hire? This is where you tell them something about you as an individual that will pique their interest in talking to you.

Imagine that you are about to purchase a large, expensive appliance that you expect to use for several years. You would want to know as much as you can about the quality of the product and as much as you could learn about what it is made from and how it was put together. If you were to look at a brochure about this particular apparatus, you might see words such as:

- Efficient

- Effective

- Affordable

- Stylish

- Durable

If you saw those words, you probably would not get particularly excited. They are nice words, but rather dull. However, what if the description of this appliance included a little extra "juice" in the descriptions and said something like:

- Provides maximum efficiency compared to other brands

- Exemplary performance

- Tremendous value

- Blends wonderfully with any decor

- Built to last

Keep in mind that in your job search, you are the product and your resume is your brochure. You have to provide the "juice" that catches the reader's attention and separates you from the crowd. Also remember that in a buyer's market the rules are different than in a seller's market. It is not enough to have a skill set. There are probably lots of people who can do the same things that you can do, and maybe even do them better. Companies are looking for people who can not only perform the task well, but also who can do it in such a way that helps those around them be more productive and good in their jobs.

Before we go too far in using descriptive terminology, understand that you should never describe yourself in such a way that is not an accurate representation of who you really are. Even if you like the sound of the phrase, do not use it unless it is accurate in describing you. The trick is in knowing what describes you that will be appealing to the person who reads your resume.

How do you know what those qualities are that are an accurate representation of you? One way is to ask those who know you best to be brutally honest with you and to tell you what they perceive your best qualities are to them. Keep in mind however, that you are not going to get an impartial, objective response from them even though they may try to offer it as such. Their responses will be affected, to at least some degree, by their relationship with you, good or bad.

Another way to do it is to use one of the totally objective personality assessment tools that are offered by several sources, such as school placement offices, professional counselors and therapists, and some career counselors. The tool that I like is the DISC Personality Assessment. By answering twenty four questions in a timed environment, you will get a printed report that is an incredibly accurate gauge of how you see yourself, how others see you, and the personality you exhibit when you are in a stressful circumstance. It shows who you are at your core, in other words.

Another good one is the Myers-Briggs assessment tool. It is been around a long time and has a good reputation as an accurate representation of personality type. You should not have any problems finding several providers who can offer one or several of these personality assessment tools. These tools will tell you not only the qualities that best describe you, but also the degree to which they apply to you.

Whichever tool you use, the results will give you what you need to put on your resume as a description of who you are and what qualities you can offer to the benefit of the organization that you are interested in joining. Now comes the part where you begin a significant departure from the standard resume. Do not be afraid to think (and speak) "out of the box." If your report from the personality assessment says that you score highly in the categories of tenacity, enthusiasm, and organization, use phrases such as:

- Bulldog tenacity

- Contagious enthusiasm

- Meticulously organized

Phrases like these create a mental picture in the mind of the reader that breaks the monotony of the standard, common resumes that everyone else is submitting. No matter what kind of job you are pursuing, there are some common, universally admired qualities that hiring managers want to see in candidates. Others include (but are not limited to):

- punctual

- creative

- resilient

- dependable

- adaptable

- quick learner

- learns from mistakes

- "whatever it takes" attitude

- steady

- works well under pressure

If you are high in any of these categories, put them in your resume below the "Professional Summary" or "Objective" statement. Add qualifiers such as "very", "consistently", "unfailingly", or other strong modifiers to those characteristics that describe you, then write a sentence describing how that particular quality is revealed in how you work. For example, you might say:

"Extremely organized: Adept at bringing order out of chaos." List four or five qualities like that as bullet points, followed by a short, concise description. By doing so you will encourage the reader to continue reading to learn even more about you. You are beginning to paint a picture of who you are, which is a very important component of the resume in a buyer's market.

A good description and heading for this section is "Core Competencies." Not only is it an accurate description of what you are telling them about yourself, it also reminds the reader that you bring important benefits to their organization, which is an important consideration in choosing the candidates that they want to interview.

Chapter 4

What Have You Done and Why Does It Matter?

Let's assume that you have just graduated from college and that you are considering going to graduate school, or maybe law school, or medical school. You have a degree and you have had your school send a copy of your transcript to the graduate school where you want to continue your education. As a courtesy to the school, you send them a letter to let them know that you plan on enrolling soon, and you have included in the letter a few questions about the school. Among those questions is a very important one that you need answered so that you can finalize your plans. You simply ask, "When do I start?"

In a couple of weeks you get a reply from the school that says, in a matter-of-fact manner, "Not so fast...you first have to take an admissions test before we decide to admit you." The fact that you earned a degree from your college is nice, but they want to know more than just that. They want to know what you learned while you were there, how well you did compared to others, and quite a bit about how you think. To them, it is not enough that you simply have a piece of paper proving that you graduated. They want to know how your experience in your previous school prepared you to enter this one.

We all understand why schools require evidence that you can do well in their environment, and we accept that they have every right to make judgments based on what they learn from the admissions tests. When it comes to the hiring process however, we rarely consider that employers want to know just as much about us as the schools we want to attend. Most people completely ignore this when they construct their resume, and the result is that the reader is left to think, "So Susan worked at XYZ company as an engineer. So what?"

What the employer wants to know about Susan, in addition to the fact that she worked at XYZ company as an engineer, is what Susan learned in her time at XYZ that will bring value to her new employer when she moves. It is not enough to say what you did. You have to tell the employer why your experience will benefit them.

One of the most common questions I hear from clients is based on their concern that they have not had jobs with impressive titles, such as manager of this, or vice president of that. They tend to think that the status of their titles is what will impress the reader. Certainly titles may convey some impression of merit or accomplishment, but they are not even close to being the whole story. If you are a young job seeker especially, impressive titles may even work against you. It has become more and more common in organizations today to give out titles in lieu of bonuses or salary increases. If your background is from a very small company, employers also recognize that being vice president of this or that is irrelevant, thinking that everybody is somebody in a small organization.

One new graduate whom I worked with a few years ago was concerned that his limited work experience would work against him in his job search. While in school he had several part-time jobs and worked his way through college. His jobs included employment as the assistant manager at a sandwich shop and distributing a business newspaper to several locations throughout the city once a week. Neither of those jobs, he thought, would impress anyone. I told him that maybe the jobs were not the precursor to the executive suite in his next move, but the skills and values he learned in them certainly had value to another employer. We started listing what he had learned in those part time positions, and came up with a very valuable list of transferable skills and values that any employer would find to be beneficial. Among them were:

1. Listening skills

2. Customer service

3. Patience

4. Punctuality

5. Organization and planning

6. Training others

7. Communication skills

8. Perseverance

9. Dependability

10. Conflict resolution

11. Quality control

12. Sales

13. Empathy

14. Prioritization

15. Multi-tasking

These skills and attributes would be valuable to any employer, but they will not have any idea that you have them unless you say so in your resume. The best way to do that is to include this information in the "Experience" section of your resume. In chronological order with the most recent position first, state where you worked, your position, and the beginning month/year and ending month/year. Following this information, write a brief description of your responsibilities. Finally, add a sentence or two that tells the reader what skills you used and/or learned in carrying out those responsibilities. An example may say "Success in this position required creativity, perseverance, and a great deal of quality control. I also utilized and honed my training skills, delegation, time management, organization, and communication skills."

Use this format for each position you list in your experience. Whether you are a recent graduate or a seasoned veteran in the job market, the concept is the same. If you tell the prospective employer only what you have done without saying anything about what you learned and how you can bring those skills to your new position, you are telling only half the story and you are reducing your chances of being considered for the position.

How far back should you go in listing your experience? If you are a recent graduate, list the jobs you had while you were in school or during summer/holiday breaks. If you have been out of school for a while, go back ten years. Anything prior to that is most likely irrelevant.

While listing your job history and experience is a critical part of the resume, it can also be a source of confusion and concern. The reason is a simple one. Most employers are very cautious in considering candidates who have had several jobs in a short amount of time. They want to avoid "job hoppers." When a company makes a hiring decision they are committing to a significant expense for the future. They understand that in most cases it will be a while (weeks, maybe months) before the newly hired employee will be productive. Formal training may be involved, which can be very expensive. Perhaps as important as any cost they will incur is the opportunity cost of not hiring someone else. If they hire you and you do not work out, they have invested a significant sum in you and will receive little or nothing in return for it. So, it is understandable that they want to be comfortable with the decision to put you on the payroll instead of someone else.

However, if your resume shows that you have had multiple jobs within a short time period (say, four or five jobs in five years), they see a red flag. It is almost universal that everyone gets a pass on their first job. While there are some who find their bliss in their first job and stay in it for a long time, most people stay in it for one or two years and move on after they have a clearer picture of what they want to do. In general, the younger you are the more leeway you have in having a few jobs in a short time period. Most employers are empathetic and remember that it may have taken them a few tries to find the right position as well. As you get older and more experienced however, moving from one job to another with a few months in one and a few months in another, maybe a year in one position and then moving again, will be an additional challenge for you in seeking a new position.

Are there exceptions? Certainly, but you should be prepared to give good reasons why you may have moved from one job to another. Most employers tend to think that your past is a pretty good indicator of your future, and they do not want to be on your resume as another former employer in a short period of time.

What are those exceptions? There are some people who have just been unlucky in their job history. If you have a long work history with one company, and a subsequent succession of short-term positions in an area that has been especially affected by the downturns in the economy, most employers will be more forgiving about a high number of job changes. I have worked with several people who live in the upper Midwest, where the local economies were heavily dependent on the automobile industry. When the car companies started laying off workers, the momentum spread to virtually every sector of the workplace in those communities. If you have been working in an industry that was hard-hit by economic conditions that resulted in layoffs, closures, and/or shutdowns, you will not be measured by circumstances beyond your control.

Generally, if you have demonstrated a steady work history in one place or, for the more experienced worker, multi-year tenures in even two or three places and then were affected by conditions beyond your control that caused you to be unemployed or created circumstances where you had to find any kind of work you could get, you will not be looked upon as a risky hire for just those factors. It is not going to help you, but it will not be a big detriment either.

The candidate that employers want to avoid is the person who just does not seem to be able to keep a job or be satisfied when there are no extenuating circumstances behind the starts and stops in the job history.

There may be many times during your job or career search when you see or hear about an opportunity and ask yourself whether you would be qualified for the position. When companies advertise to fill a position, they usually list several specific qualifications that they want to see in the ideal candidate. It would be great if companies and recruiters could find the ideal candidate for every position, but more often than not, that is not the case. It is hard to quantify, but what happens most of the time is that a company winds up with someone who fits between eighty and ninety percent of what they want, and they hire the person and move on. The key is in knowing which factors are "cast in stone" and which ones have a little "wiggle room".

Out of all the candidates I have placed with companies over the years, and I would estimate that fewer than a dozen of them rated at ninety-five percent or better when compared to the ideal that companies list when they initiate the search. The point here is that if you see an opportunity for which you think you would be a good candidate, go for it!

Obviously, you have to understand that there are some qualifications that have no wiggle room at all. For example, if the position is one that requires a license to do the job and you do not have such a license or the capacity to get it in short order, you are not going to get that job. But if you have been preparing to take a licensing exam, or if you have taken it and just have not received the results yet, there is no reason why you should not pursue the opportunity. Quite often companies will make an accommodation to work with someone who may be just a little short of completing a qualifying task for a job if they know that the candidate will complete the task in short order.

Another factor to consider is the experience factor. If, for instance, a company states that they want someone with five year's experience, there may be some wiggle room. Ask yourself "What do they REALLY want?" There is nothing magical about five years, or ten years, or thirteen and a half years. What the company is saying is that they generally believe that five years is the amount of time that they believe it takes for a person to have accumulated the adequate skills and experience to do the job at the level that they need it done. However, there are a lot of people who can go through a five year period and learn very little, while others can gain ten years worth of skills in an intense, three or four year time period. It is different with every person and every background.

If you can show that you have the necessary skills, expertise, and knowledge that the job requires and that you gained it in three and a half years of intense work and devotion to the task, that may be enough to get you an interview and a job offer. I see this quite often in sales jobs. Some people are just naturally gifted sales people. They have the drive, ambition, perseverance, and "people" skills necessary for success in sales positions before they ever start a sales job. Others who do not have any of those qualities may not be as qualified for a position even with ten years of experience.

The real key in listing your experience is to point out how it can translate into benefits for your prospective employer. They want to see how what you did in your other positions can bring value to them.

Every recruiter has clients who have biases, prejudices, preferences, blind spots, and irrational attitudes with regard to the candidates they like to see. I have had them, and in my conversations with other recruiters, I know that they have them as well. And it should come as no big surprise that some hiring authorities in some companies have these attitudes as well. I am not trying to justify it, but simply to say that human nature being what it is, everyone is not viewed through the same lenses when considering candidates for positions.

My own prejudice is towards people who either cannot spell or will not use the myriad of tools available to them to avoid spelling errors. If I see a resume or a cover letter with a misspelled word, I discard it. Rationally, I understand that anyone can make a typo, and I know that I have made my share of them in my own written communications (you might even see an example in this book!), but poor spelling in a cover letter or resume indicates to me a lack of professionalism on the part of the writer, and I am not willing to take a chance on that person by sending them to one of my corporate clients. That attitude has probably cost me some pretty good candidates who may have been hired, but that is an area where I draw a line in the sand.

There are state and federal laws on the books that make it illegal to discriminate against a person on the basis of race, ethnicity, religion, age, and many other factors, but do not for a minute think that discrimination is not alive and well in the workplace. It exists, and it will always exist, so the real question is how to deal with it. The best way to deal with it is for you to be as discriminating ("picky") about the jobs you pursue as companies are about the people they hire. Every organization has its own personality. Within industries each organization has a reputation that is known to all the others in that industry, as well as to most outsiders. The first and best thing you can do is to be qualified for the job, but if that is not an issue, understand that they are going to hire the one that they like the best, and that can be influenced by any number of factors. Just as it may be difficult for you to pinpoint why your friends and you mesh well together, companies and their people are the same way. I have seen companies not hire people who had the required skills and experience because they felt it was not a good fit and not be able to explain specifically what did not feel right, and I have seen candidates reject job offers from companies that needed what they could offer for the same reason, and both of them were probably right. Pressed for specific reasons, it was difficult to pinpoint why it was not a good fit, but when your internal radar tells you that the compatibility is not there, it is probably correct.

In all my years in the recruiting industry, the people who seem to have had the most difficult time landing the jobs they sought have been a part of one or more of several groups. Each has their own specific challenges, and for each there is a bad news / good news way to view it.

At the top of the list is the "Over Fifty" crowd. In difficult economic times, you can lower that age to forty. The bad news for the over-fifty job seeker is that some companies reason that they can hire someone younger who will come in at a lower salary. The cost to the company is lower at the outset, but they are taking a chance that the younger worker will not be as productive as someone more experienced. Companies also reason that a younger worker has not been trained in ways that may not be compatible with the company's way of doing things, so there are no bad habits to break. For outside sales jobs where the travel can grind a person down over a long period of time, many companies prefer a younger person who has not seen the downside of business travel. If a young person is put into a sales position that involves travel, it may be a big adventure to them for quite a while, at least until they have been everywhere two or three times and the glamour of flying and hotels begins to fade.

The good news for the over-fifty crowd is that the first wave of baby-boomers is beginning to retire, and there are fewer workers in younger demographic groups to take their places. Prior to the recession that began in the last half of 2008, forecasters were projecting worker shortages in many industries. The recession and the accompanying disappearance of many retirement nest eggs has prompted many who planned to retire to delay that retirement, but as time goes by and the baby boomers become a smaller part of the workforce, there will be a renewed appreciation for the older workers. Many companies are beginning to discover that hiring older workers can produce unexpected benefits, and some of their fears, such as higher medical coverage costs, are not necessarily occurring. They have found that, for the most part, the older workers can become productive faster than younger, less experienced workers, that they tend to show up for work on a regular basis, on time, and their experience often leads to increased productivity for the company.

As the trend for people to live longer, healthier, more active lives continues, many companies and most workers are beginning to re-think what retirement really means. There are still challenges for the older worker who wants to re-enter the workforce or change jobs, but the long-term trends are favorable. For the immediate future however, the key for the more experienced worker is to emphasize the value of the experience they bring to the job, the shorter learning curve, and that the company can count on them to be there every day.

Some candidates, aware that age discrimination is alive and well, go to great lengths to avoid providing any information that might reveal how old they are prior to a face-to-face interview, thinking that if they can just get the interview they can overcome any age prejudices that they might encounter. One commonly employed tactic is to provide a job history that goes back only a few years and not to put a graduation date on the education section of the resume. Discrimination in hiring on the basis of age is a violation of federal law, as well as the law of all states, but proving that a person's age is the reason that a job offer did not materialize is not an open and shut case. Leaving the date off the resume will prevent the recruiter or hiring manager from "doing the math", but they are so used to looking at this information on resumes that when it is not there, it usually raises a red flag for the reader. It also tends to make it look like the candidate is trying to hide something, so most recruiters and hiring managers will simply discard the resume. As a rule of thumb, I advise full disclosure and honesty rather than subtle attempts to hide what is going to come out sooner or later anyway. You cannot predict or control someone else's outlook or whether they have any discriminatory attitudes. What you can do is focus on the value and benefits you can bring to the organization, and make sure that your resume and your interview performance exemplify them. Do not spend time worrying about things that you cannot change. When you focus on the negative, your attitude reflects your thinking and it will come out in your demeanor. Instead, focus on the factors that you can affect. You will find that by doing so your own outlook will be more positive and it will go a long way toward minimizing the effect of whatever you were worrying about in the first place.

Most positions that companies need to fill have some criteria that are absolutely required, but more often than not there is some degree of flexibility in at least some of those requirements. What is rarely communicated to candidates is that there are "hard" requirements, and there are "soft" requirements. As long as you are a good fit in the hard ones, there is a good chance that the factors where you may fall outside the ideal fit may have some flexibility. For example, a written job description may say that five years experience is required, but most companies recognize that a person who is exceptionally talented may be every bit as qualified with three years of intense, excellent experience as someone else may be with five years of less intense experience, especially if the person with three years experience has met and overcome significant challenges and has excelled in the job performance in that three years. The longer the company has been looking for the right person, the more likely they are to be flexible in some areas of the job description.

Another group faces challenges that may exceed even those in the "over fifty" crowd. I am speaking of mothers with young children. Perhaps no group is as universally and unfairly discriminated against as this group. "Phobia" is perhaps too strong a word, but many companies are very reluctant to put mothers of young children on the payroll. The reason why is fairly obvious. The perception is that young children get sick a lot, and in our culture it is generally assumed, for right or wrong, that the mother is going to stay home with the sick child. Companies do not want to hire someone whom they think cannot be relied upon to show up for work on a regular basis. That is the bad news.

The good news is that many long over-due changes are occurring in the workplace. Women are rising to positions of significant authority in many organizations, including the CEO ranks. Our graduate schools, law schools, medical schools, and other professional schools are becoming increasingly more populated with women...in many cases more than fifty percent. Many companies, whether they are headed by men or women, are making a much more serious effort at following not only the letter, but also the spirit of the law with regards to discrimination. Additionally, the traditional roles of mom and dad in the family are changing. While still not the norm, it is becoming more and more common for stay-at-home dads to take care of the house and kids while mom works.

More and more companies are also very reluctant to hire people who smoke, again citing health care costs as a reason for their stance. Others have told me that people who do not smoke tend to resent the smoking breaks taken by those who do smoke, which can cause discord in the work environment. Some studies have indicated that there is a higher rate of absenteeism for smokers compared to the workers who do not smoke. The anti-smoking movement seems to be gathering momentum in all quarters, and some companies have established policies that state that if you smoke, even if it is only when you are not on the job, it is grounds for termination. If you do smoke, certainly it would be to your benefit to quit, but at the very least you should avoid smoking prior to a job interview. Some people find the odor of smoke very offensive, and there is no good reason to take that chance.

Because of the high cost of making a hiring mistake, more and more companies are doing thorough background checks on candidates that they are interested in hiring. My own experience, which has been confirmed by many studies done by other groups, suggests that more than fifty percent of resumes have "enhanced" or downright false information on them. Most of these "enhancements" are in the area of claiming a degree that does not really exist, or inflating the title and/or responsibilities of a previous position. I have seen resumes that had outright lies in them regarding where a person worked or what they did at the organization where they claim to have been employed. One of the most common falsifications is to state that a person worked at a particular company for longer than they really worked there.

The Internet is filled with offers of degrees from online "universities" that will issue you a diploma for your "life experiences." Coincidentally, the higher your degree, the more it costs. Bachelor's degrees can be had for as little as one hundred dollars, while a PhD may cost upwards of three to four hundred dollars. Admittedly, some people have gotten away with this type of fraud (at least so far), but more and more companies are becoming diligent about verifying education and work experience. In most cases, when this falsification is discovered, it is grounds for immediate termination.

Checking the credit of a candidate is becoming almost commonplace for companies today. They want to know how well you handle your finances before they put you in a position of responsibility in their organization, and this caution is not just in regards to positions that handle money within the company. The common thinking is that how you handle your money is a good indicator of how well you handle other responsibilities as well. Do your best to keep your credit in good shape, as it will come back to haunt you in the job search if you have a poor credit record.

Criminal background checks are the norm these days, and drug testing is commonplace. You should assume that you will be subject to both of these investigations, and be surprised if they do not happen.

If you are interested in a job that involves driving on company business, whether it is in your car or in a vehicle provided by the company, you should be ready for a thorough check of your driving record. The carnage on the road caused by drunk drivers is a major priority for law enforcement today. Organizations such as MADD (Mothers Against Drunk Driving) have pushed DUI offenses to the top of the list for law enforcement, and the penalties are severe. One DUI offense is a red flag, and anything more than that can really hurt your chances of meaningful employment. In most states, getting a job is the least of your worries if you have had more than one DUI, especially if they are within ten years of each other. In general, my experience with companies is that the further back the violation is in your past, the less of a negative factor it will be in considering you for employment. Additionally, the younger you were when you got it, the better for you as well, especially if a few years have passed since the violation and no more citations have followed it. I cannot speak for every company, but most of those I have worked with have had the attitude that most young people make foolish choices once in a while, and some of them get caught and pay a stiff penalty. Everyone makes mistakes, but the key is whether the offender learned a lesson and did not repeat the offense.

One last warning is appropriate. Social networking is part of the fabric of our society today, and most people have profiles on multiple sites such as Facebook, LinkedIn, MySpace, and others. Companies realize this, and are not at all hesitant to see how you present yourself to the world on these sites. How you tell the world who you are on these sites can have a big impact on your candidacy for a job. Your circle of friends or relatives may have some understanding of why you could have photos and/or language on your site that may not be suitable for young children, but your attempt at humor to your friends may cost you a job. You are certainly free to put on your site anything that the hosting rules permit, but you should do so with the understanding that some who view it may not find it amusing or acceptable. If you are serious about getting a job and your site is replete with dubious language and photos, clean it up. What may seem like innocent fun to you and your friends may be construed as inappropriate by someone who does not know you. You may never know whether your information has cost you the chance to be considered for a job. It is not uncommon for recruiters and HR professionals at companies to look at these sites as part of a preliminary investigation into someone as a candidate for a position. If what they see is objectionable, you may be disregarded before you even knew you were considered.

So here is the real caveat for any candidate to consider. Understand that companies are picky about not only whether you can do the job, but also what kind of person you are, and they will do all that they can to get a good idea of who you really are if you want to work for them. The stakes are too high not to do everything they can to avoid a hiring mistake. Make sure that you make every effort to not have any red flags pop up when they try to dig into who you really are.

Chapter 5

The Interview

I mentioned earlier that the recruiting business can be described as an industrial dating service. Two parties may notice each other through various means, and when one of them gets interested enough in the other, the interested party contacts the other one to see about setting up a first date. That is where you are in this process now. You have noticed the company or organization that interests you, and you have taken the initiative to contact them, either directly or through your recruiter, and now you have an initial meeting set up to see if you like each other enough to go forward and establish a relationship.

And just like in that first date scenario in your social life, how things go on that first meeting will determine if there are second and subsequent meetings and any chance at all of a long-term relationship. There are myriad reasons why this may be a challenging and stressful experience. I had a coach in high school who repeatedly reminded us that "You will play like you practice", and he was right. How you prepare for this experience will have everything to do with how you perform during the interview.

You do not want to blow it, and if you will follow the guidelines that I will lay out for you, you will set yourself up for subsequent interviews and perhaps a job offer.

These suggestions are appropriate for most interviews. I will cover some of them more specifically later, but familiarize yourself with each of them before you arrive for the interview.

1. Arrive a few minutes early. I suggest getting there around ten minutes before the scheduled time. *Know the name of the person you are there to see!* You'd be surprised how many people forget who to ask for when they arrive.

2. You will probably meet a few other people before you meet the interviewer. A receptionist is likely to be the first person you meet. Have a smile and a pleasant word for everyone you meet. It is very likely that the interviewer will ask others who met you what they think about you. I have seen a lot of candidates derail their chances because they were so focused on meeting the interviewer that they either did not notice others or disregarded everyone else who was there. What they did not realize was that other people would weigh in on the hiring decision, either formally or informally.

3. Turn off your cell phone! You do not want it ringing or vibrating in your pocket or purse. It is a distraction and it signals to the interviewer that you did not do a good job of preparing before you arrived.

4. Bring a few copies of your resume in case the interviewer or other people you may meet want to see it. Most of the time the interviewer will have already reviewed it and probably will not ask for it, but it is a good thing to have just in case.

5. Prepare yourself ahead of time by learning what you can about the company. You should know something about the history of the company, its products and/or services, revenues, reputation, the market(s) they serve, and any outstanding accomplishments they are known for in the public eye. You should also know something about the culture of the organization and how they compare to others in the same field or industry. If the company is publicly held, you can get a lot of information about them from their annual report and other sources that are available online. If the company is privately held, you can still get information by asking others you know

and putting the name of the company into search engines online. However you do it, learn all you can about them.

6. Ask for the interviewer's business card...*very* important. Ask for one from everyone you meet while at their offices. You may think you will remember everyone's name, but you will not.

7. Understand going into the interview that the primary task of the interviewer is to determine whether you can do the job. It will not matter a bit how smooth and polished you are in your presentation skills if you do not have the skills and experience to effectively carry out the responsibilities of the job. Be ready to explain how and why you can do the job by citing examples of how you have accomplished similar tasks in your previous or other positions.

8. The secondary task of the interviewer is to determine whether you will fit well with those who already work there. If the interviewer does not like you, you are not going to get the job. The process of the interviewer deciding whether he or she likes you begins when they first see you. Go back to the advice your mother gave you when you went to school. Stand up straight, shoulders back, smile, and offer a firm (not bone crushing) handshake.

9. Start out by saying that you have been looking forward to the interview and that you appreciate the opportunity to meet the interviewer and discuss the job.

10. Be sure that you look the interviewer in the eye when you are talking. People do not generally view someone else favorably if they do not have good eye contact. If you are staring out the window or looking at something else in the office while speaking to the interviewer, it indicates a lack of confidence on your part and is a definite mark against you.

11. Have some good questions prepared to ask about the organization. Ask about the culture...what type person fits it best. Ask specific questions about the job responsibilities. Look

professional by bringing a business "organizer" or notebook, and have your questions written in it. Generally the type that has an 8 ½" x 11" tablet in it is best. Get a dark colored one…black or burgundy. You can get one at Office Depot or some other office supply house for about $10.

12. The interviewer will likely ask you open-ended questions that are designed to get you to talk in other than "yes" or "no" answers. Be prepared to tell the interviewer why you are successful and have some examples of how and why you have been successful in your current or past positions.

13. Be aware that for every question you are asked, there is a hidden agenda for asking it. The interviewer in interested not only in what you say, but in how well you say it. Are your thoughts organized? Do you get rattled easily? Do you speak with confidence?

14. Remember that organizations are not interested in average performers. They want all-stars who have a "whatever it takes" attitude…a "fire in the belly" quality that separates average performers from everyone else. I do not know where the line is that separates enthusiasm from being cocky and overly exuberant, but get as close to that line as you can without crossing over it. You have to let the interviewer know that you enjoy a challenge and that you have high performance standards for yourself.

15. Emphasize your communications skills and your human relations skills and experience. Most jobs, more than anything else, are about how well someone works with other people.

16. Understand that you will probably have contact with people at every level of the organization. Your boss should know that you can work effectively with people at any level.

17. Dress appropriately…coat and tie for the interview for guys…suit for the ladies…and shine your shoes! Most jobs have a casual dress code once you get the job, but for the

interview you should dress like a professional. If the job is clearly one in which "casual" is the dress code, then at least show up neatly dressed and groomed. You want your interviewer to think that you put some thought and effort into your preparation and appearance. If you are in doubt about the dress code, err on the high side. It is better to be overdressed than underdressed.

18. At the end of the interview, ask some kind of closing question to let him/her know you are interested in moving forward. The interviewer will be looking for some kind of indication of interest from you and may figure that if you do not pursue the job, you are probably not that interested. You can tell the interviewer that you know a lot about the organization already, and that you had a very favorable impression of the organization before you came to the interview. Then follow up by saying that all your favorable impressions have been confirmed in the interview, and that you are very interested in moving forward in the process. Ask how the interview process works and when you can expect to hear something about any next steps in the process. Be sure you are telling the truth when you tell them these things. If you do not feel that way and are not interested, do not say that you are. Just express your appreciation for the opportunity to interview and exit gracefully.

19. Do not discuss the compensation issue unless the interviewer brings it up. If you like them and they like you, that will be a topic for the next meeting. The first interview is usually a "get to know you" type of meeting for both sides. If they do bring up the compensation issue you should be ready to discuss it, but for you to bring it up makes you look like the money is the only factor that is important to you. If the job is one for which the compensation is already a fixed, non-negotiable sum, it is more likely to be a part of the conversation than if it is a negotiable element of the interview process.

20. Do not ever say anything negative about current or previous employers, no matter how tempting it is to do so, even if everything you could say is true. Doing so almost always leaves a bad impression with the interviewer. They will think that if you talk negatively about former employers, you will do the same thing about them someday.

21. No profanity or off-color humor…ever. There is no upside to it, and the only outcome you can expect is negative.

22. Avoid crutch phrases ("you know…", "like…", "Um, Um…"). This will take some practice on your part as well as the cooperation of a few friends or relatives who know you well and can point out how you use these phrases. No matter how well you think you know your own mannerisms, habits, and language patterns, you do not. Trust me on that. Get input from others and work on it.

23. Just as most of us have some crutch phrases that we are not aware of, most of us also have gestures, postures, and facial expressions that define us as well. If you have any habits that are distracting to those you are talking to, learn what they are and practice talking without using them. I am not saying "Do not smile" or do not use your hands at all when you are talking, but if any of your body language shouts that you are uncomfortable or distracting to the person you are talking to, you will do yourself a big favor by being aware of it and reducing your dependence on it.

24. When you leave the interview, on the same day, write a "thank you" e-mail and send it or a hand-written note and mail it to the interviewer and to anyone else from whom you received a business card. A hand-written note is always preferable to an e-mail, but only if it gets there the next day. I suggest carrying the note card with you, writing the note after you leave the interview, and mailing it immediately. If you know that the person is about to leave on a trip or be gone from the office for an extended period, send an e-mail instead. It is likely that the

interviewer will have access to e-mail whether in the office or not.

25. When you get out of the interview, compare your post-interview impressions to your pre-interview impressions of the company and the job. Do an objective, analytical (it is best if you do it on paper) appraisal of the opportunity and consider whether you can be happy in the job. If you are not happy in your job, the money does not matter.

Preparing for the interview experience gives you a two-fold advantage. The first is that by preparing ahead of time you will be ready in each of the specific areas that you have anticipated. The other advantage, and just as important, is that pre-interview preparation will give you a quiet confidence that you are going to do well. That confidence will come through in how you are perceived by the interviewer and will work to your advantage throughout the interview.

Chapter 6

Those Pesky Questions

When you arrive at the interview, greet the interviewer, and then sit down, it is a foregone conclusion that the two of you are not going to just sit there and stare at each other. There is going to be a dialogue between the two of you, and most of it is going to be the interviewer asking questions and you answering them. You will also be expected to ask some questions, but they will generally be after the interviewer has asked you several questions.

You will be asked two basic types of questions, both of which have more than one purpose. As I stated earlier, the interviewer is interested in not only what you say, but how well you say it. It is not only the content of your responses, but also the skill and comfort you display when you give those responses that will matter to the interviewer. In other words, it is not just your knowledge, but also your communications skills that matter.

More than any other part of the interview process, this dialogue will determine whether there will be any next steps in bringing you into the organization. While every interview is unique and can go in any direction, there are some basic caveats that you should be aware of going in that can help you maximize your positive impact on the interviewer.

The first critical task for you is to *listen* well. There are several reasons why. One is that people (and interviewers are people) love to talk about themselves. There is no guarantee that the person who interviews you will be a skilled and experienced interviewer. They may be as nervous as you are and be completely disorganized, and you have to be ready for that circumstance. Unskilled or inexperienced interviewers often place their questions for you within stories about themselves. They may not even ask you a direct question. Instead, you may hear a story about something that they did or experienced and then the story will stop. It is up to you to decide whether you are supposed to dig out the "implied" question from this performance and offer you own opinion or response to it. Sometimes the interviewer is just looking for affirmation from you that you understand what they are saying. This is most likely to occur at the beginning of the interview. Some people feel like they have to establish their own credibility to you before they begin talking to you about why you are interested in the job and would be a good fit for it. This may not happen, but it is not uncommon. Just be aware that the person who interviews you may or may not be a skilled and prepared interviewer.

Assuming that the interviewer is as prepared as you should be, be ready for questions that are designed to address two critical areas of interest to the interviewer. Those are (1) Can you do the job? and (2) Will you fit in well with the people who already work there? Every question you get will have one or both of those agendas as a purpose. The most common complaints I hear from corporate clients with regard to the question/answer portion of the interview is that the candidate rambles too much in the answer and that they start talking before the interviewer finishes asking the question.

Both of these conditions come from nervous tension, and you have to be able to control it. There is a difference between crippling nervous tension and enthusiasm. The latter is encouraged, but the former is an interview killer. Quite often the candidate is so focused on what he or she wants to say that they do not listen to what the interviewer is asking. That is why it is so important to listen well and to make sure you understand the questions. It is perfectly acceptable to pause for a moment or two before beginning to answer the question. If you need to organize your thoughts, it is better to take a moment to plan what you are going to say than to just start babbling and hope that something intelligent comes out of your mouth. When you start babbling, you know it, the interviewer knows it, and the more you talk, the less sense you make. It is an uncomfortable situation for both parties. So, pause for a moment to plan what want to say. I am not saying that you should sit there for two minutes with a confused look on your face, but a brief pause to plan your response provides two benefits to you. First, it helps you craft an intelligent, appropriate response. Second, it makes you appear to be a person who is not too quick to pull the trigger when you have a decision to make. That can be beneficial in how you are perceived by the interviewer.

If the question does not make sense, or you are not sure exactly what the interviewer is asking, ask for clarification. A simple query such as, "I want to be sure I completely understand the question. Can you elaborate just a bit?" is perfectly reasonable. Once you fully understand the question, you will be much more comfortable in crafting your answer. Another good reason for a pause is that the interviewer may not be finished talking. A brief pause on your part will ensure that it is your turn to talk. You have to very careful in this situation because you are likely to be excited or nervous, and maybe you just cannot wait to say what you want say. A few seconds can seem like an eternity when you are excited, but do not let your excitement overcome your good sense.

While some questions that you will receive may be technical in nature and will focus on your skills and experience, others will likely be more targeted towards learning about your personality, your communications skills, and your ability to "think on your feet." You may not get every one of these questions thrown at you, but chances are very good that you will be asked a few of them in one form or another. Here is list of several of the most common interview questions, along with the type of answer that you should be ready to give when you hear these questions:

1. *So, tell me about yourself!*

    This is not so much a question, but rather an invitation for you to give the interviewer a condensed version of your background and the reasons for your interest in the job. The interviewer is not looking for your autobiography. This also serves as an ice-breaker question...a chance for you to warm up a little and for the interviewer to get a basic idea of how well you express yourself. Do not launch into a ten minute dissertation. A statement or two about where you grew up, where you went to school, the jobs you have had (with most of the focus on your most recent position), and why you are on the career path you have chosen is sufficient. If the interviewer wants to know anything else, they can ask you, but do not venture into the personal side (marriage status, kids, hobbies, etc...) unless you are asked specifically about those topics. The experienced interviewers know not to ask those questions, as they can be construed as delving into information that could be used as a basis for prejudice against you.

2.   *Where do you want to be in five years?*

You may be tempted to say "on the beach in Maui!" but control yourself. This question has been asked by more interviewers more times for more years than just about any other interview question, and while it is still common, it is going out of style. The reason is the same as the answer you will give. Your reply should go something like this: "It is hard to say what specific position I'd want, considering how fast business and technology are changing and continue to evolve, but whatever my specific job, I want to be doing something that is challenging and rewarding, that makes me look forward to getting up in the morning, and that makes a positive difference in how well my company does in the marketplace. I want to be a difference maker." There are a lot of jobs today that did not even exist five years ago, and most of it is due to advancement in technology. You also have no way of knowing what condition the company will be in five years in the future or if it will even exist in its current form. The truth is that no one has any idea what they will be doing or where they will be doing it in two years, five years, or twelve years. Your best answer is one that does not make you appear to be out of touch with reality.

3.   *Tell me what you know about this job and what you think it involves.*

This is one of those questions that you should prepare for ahead of time. Do your homework so that you really do have a good understanding of what the job involves and whether you think you are a good fit. Your answer should be brief and focused on what you know about the responsibilities and activities in the job. More people stumble on this question than just about any other question they will hear. The reason they stumble is that they go into the interview thinking, "I am smart and I can figure out whatever I do not know." However, the interviewer wants to hear specific information that relates to the particular job you are discussing. If you try to fake your way through it by speaking in vague generalities, the interviewer will know immediately that you have no clue what you are talking about, and your chances of getting the job drop significantly. If you are seeking a job that has been posted in a public forum, such as a posting on one of the Internet job boards, there will be at least a basic description of the job in the posting. If you are working through a recruiter, that recruiter should be able to give you all the information you will need to understand exactly what the job is and what it requires. If you do have a pretty good idea of what the job is about but you still have some questions, say what you know and then ask a few questions about what you do not know. The interviewer will not expect you to know everything, but do not show up knowing nothing!

4.   *What do you know about this company/organization?*

A poor answer on this one will eliminate you from consideration faster than any other question. Some interviewers have told me that they feel insulted when the reply they get is something like, "Not much." I like this question because it has brought me more recruiting business from frustrated managers than any other question. After a few interviews in which the interviewer hears some inane comments or sees a puzzled look on the faces of a few candidates, I get calls asking me to "Find me some good candidates. I do not have time to meet with more clowns." It would be easier to understand why people do not do well with this question if the information was hard to find, but that is not the case. If the company is publicly traded, it is easy to do an Internet search to learn about the company. You can get copies of their annual report or look up articles in the news or in trade magazines. Ask around. If you know what they sell, talk to some of their customers to get an idea of how the company is viewed in their industry. At a minimum, you should know what industry the company is in, the specific products or services they offer, what position (relative to competitors) they hold in the business in terms of market share, and any recent news about the company that was in the public domain.

5.   *Why do you want to work here?*

The most brutally honest answer is "I am not sure that I do...that is why I am here...to learn more about the organization and see if it is a good fit." While it may be honest, it also comes across as a bit haughty, so your best bet is to tone it down. A good interviewer will understand and acknowledge that the interview process is a two-way exercise. You are interviewing them every bit as much as they are interviewing you, and it is not a good fit unless it is a good fit both ways. A good way to express that perspective is to say something like, "I have researched several companies that I think might be a good fit for my skills and experience. What I have been able to learn about this company tells me that it is a leader in the field and well-respected in the industry, and that is the kind of company I want to join. I hope to learn more today, and I appreciate this opportunity to meet with you."

If this company is involved in something that you are really passionate about, say so. For example, if the company is involved in the "green" movement, making products that preserve the environment, and you are really interested in that field, tell the interviewer why you are so interested. If it is the truth, your enthusiasm will come through in your conversation and be apparent to the interviewer, and that can only help your candidacy for the job.

6.   *Tell me why you are the person we should hire.*

This is a very common question, and you should be prepared for it with a good answer. This is your opportunity to blow your own horn. It is like the pitcher has just thrown you a beach ball down the middle of the plate, so you should be ready to knock it out of the park. It is essential to have good eye contact when you offer this answer. If you are looking down or out the window, you give the impression that do not really believe what you are saying. Lean forward a little and say "Everything I have learned about this organization tells me that you are committed to quality in your products and services. That does not come from hiring mediocre people. I have the energy, creativity, skills, and work ethic that can help you excel in your business, and I am looking for the opportunity to do that." This is not the time to be modest, but it is not the time to overstate your qualifications either. If you do not believe it, you should not be there.

7. *Why are you available?*

This question can come in various form. You may hear, "Why are you interested in making a job change? Or, "Why are you in the market for another job?" However you hear it, it is the same question and it is likely that you will hear it in one form or another. As with most of the other questions you will hear, the truth is the best answer, but you can phrase it to your advantage. Simply state that you are currently happily employed and are not looking for a change, but that you heard about the opportunity (either from a recruiter or some other source), that the job and the company looked attractive, and that it piqued your interest. Recruiters and hiring authorities typically prefer to find candidates who are already employed, happy, well-paid, and not looking for a change. There are two good reasons for this answer. One is that it is the truth and you can say it with sincerity. The other is that the interviewer realizes that you are already working somewhere else, happy, and not particularly interested in making a change unless there is some compelling reason to do so. There is something about human nature that makes us want something that someone else has. If you are employed, you are more attractive than if you are not working. If the interviewer knows that you are perfectly content to stay where you are unless you have a very good reason to leave, the playing field becomes much more level. If you are interested and the interviewer is as well, both of you will do a better job of selling what you have to offer than if it is a one-sided bargaining proposition. Simply state that "I was intrigued by what I learned about this position and the company, and I would like to learn more about it."

On the other hand, if you are not working and were part of a general downsizing, say so. Tell the interviewer that you were laid off in a downsizing and cost-cutting purge, and that you are pursuing new opportunities where you can use the skills and talents that you have developed in your years in business.

If you were terminated, your best bet is to be up front and honest about it. It happens, both to good people and worthless employees. There are a lot of reasons why someone can get fired, and some are more serious than others. Getting fired does not mean that you will never get another job, but it probably does mean that you will have a more challenging task in getting that job than someone who has a "clean" record. An open-minded interviewer will probably probe to get details. If you were fired because you deserved it, do not lie about it. Lies tend to create the need for more lies, and pretty soon you have woven a web of deceit that you cannot maintain. People get fired for all kinds or reasons...personality conflicts, poor performance, and sometimes for no good reason. Your explanation to others for your firing will be affected by how well you have come to grips with it yourself. A good model for how to handle something like this is to deal with it directly and not be defensive. "I was fired after a period of time in which my boss and I could not come to agreement on how I did my job and my performance. She felt very strongly one way on some important issues, and I felt differently for reasons that felt right at the time. In retrospect, there are some things I could and should have done differently, but I learned from the experience and I am ready to move forward, wiser now and with a new perspective." An answer like this indicates that you are confident and resilient, and that you are not trying to avoid an uncomfortable part of your past.

Rest assured that your references will be checked if the prospective employer is interested in you. Find out, if you can, what your former employer will say or not say about you if contacted for a reference. There should not be any big discrepancies between your explanation and theirs. Many employers today take the position of not commenting at all on former employees, other than to confirm dates of employment. You cannot control whether they talk, but if they do, your story and theirs should be in sync.

If you were terminated for cause, you are going to have to deal with a challenging set of circumstances to gain new employment. "Cause" generally means that no notice or severance pay is due to the employee. It can spring from a number of factors, including dishonesty, theft, participation in a competitor business, insolence, and insubordination. In some cases, absenteeism for a prolonged illness or incompetence can also be considered just cause for termination. There is no upside to you for any of these reasons for termination. Employers are generally very wary of hiring someone whom they think will bring trouble or problems to the job. If you feel that you were unjustly terminated and that the cause did not exist, you have every right to explain your side of the story, but be wary. Do not launch into a persecution of your former employer. Just state the facts. If you have an otherwise sterling work history and have just one unsavory blip on your record, potential employers are much more likely to consider giving you a second chance.

A few years ago I was working with a candidate who looked like a great prospect for a sales job for one of my client companies. He was about five years out of college and had had a successful career in a middle management position. The job was one that required overnight travel two or three nights per week, and included a company car as part of the package. When I asked him if there were any skeletons in his closet that I needed to know about prior to setting up the first interview, he told me that in his senior year of college he was arrested for driving under the influence (DUI). He admitted his guilt, paid the stiff fines, served the probation, and said that he had not had another drink since his arrest. This guy was genuinely remorseful, felt terrible about his misdeed, and said that he had learned his lesson. Most companies and the people who run them, at least in my experience, are reasonable people. They understand that young people occasionally do something stupid. I advised him to tell them the same thing he told me. He did, and was offered the job. He did not take it, but he did accept another job with a different company that also offered a company car. Not only did he feel better for telling the truth, but he also was complimented for his honesty and forthrightness in admitting his mistake. In general, if you have a big mistake in your past, the "I was young, did something stupid for which I paid a steep price, learned from it, and have not repeated the mistake" explanation goes a long way in getting you on a new career path.

8.   *What are your best qualities, and what are your worst?*

Mention a few of your best attributes, one of those that you need to work on, and state that you are aware of your need to improve in the deficient area and that you take steps to not let it derail your performance. I would not advise equal time for both areas, such as "I am smart, creative, and resilient, but on the other hand I am lazy, uninspired, and obnoxious." Full disclosure will not help you in this case, and it may not even be accurate. Here is why. Most of us are much more critical of ourselves than others are. We may think that our warts and shortcomings are as obvious as a neon sign in Las Vegas, but the truth is that most people are so caught up in dealing with their own challenges that they do not dwell on those of other people. Sure, there are exceptions. There are people who find fault in others as a hobby, but that is not the majority.

A good answer may go something like this: "I am a quick learner, a great problem solver, and I am tenacious about doing the job right and completely. My biggest challenge is that I am impatient. However, I am aware that I am impatient and I consistently remind myself to be realistic about the time is takes to do some things right. Patience does not come naturally to me, but I deal with that part of my makeup by reminding myself to ease up."

9. *Describe your management style.*

This is an open-ended inquiry that usually intentionally vague. The interviewer wants to see how you handle a question that does not ask for a specific type of answer. It is an opportunity to babble incoherently or really elevate the perception that the interviewer has of you. This question may really mean, "How well do you work with other people?" and your answer should be framed in that context. The real challenge in management is in setting realistic goals and completing them though others on time and within acceptable cost parameters. Doing that requires good communications skills and the ability to make course corrections in the process. Your response should focus on planning, communication, implementation, and cost control.

10. *What are your priorities when hiring someone?*

This is an excellent question, both for the interviewer and for the candidate. The reason is that the answer will tell both of you whether you are likely to fit into the company culture smoothly. A few of the managers I have talked to about this question tend to think it can backfire on the candidate if it is answered honestly. Their reasoning is that if you say that you like to hire people who have strengths where you are not so strong, you are shooting yourself in the foot by saying that you are not good at something. A safe and honest answer is that you like to hire people who are talented, self-starters, and who work well with others. Add that it is always a priority to hire people who have the capacity to advance in the organization.

11. *Have you ever fired anyone? If so, what was that experience like for you?*

I have fired a few people in my time, and I hated it. If you have any human compassion, you will hate it too, but you have to be able to do it when the circumstances warrant termination. Once again, this question begs for an honest answer. You can say that you do not look forward to it, but you are ready to fire someone if it is necessary. Also mention that the best way is the most straightforward way. Do it and be done with it. In many cases a new start is in everyone's best interests. However, no matter how much internal justification you give yourself, the reality is that you are telling someone that they cannot come back and that you are not going to pay them anymore. State that managers are paid to make tough decisions and to implement them, and that you can do it when it is called for.

12. *When could you start if we both agree that this is a good match?*

Be very careful with this one. It is a potential booby trap. That may not be the intent when the question is asked, but it can work out that way if you do not consider your answer carefully. The answer is, it depends. It depends on several variables. First, if you are currently employed, you should state that you would need to give your current employer a reasonable notice that you are leaving. Two weeks is typical, although there may be extenuating circumstances that could allow for a shorter or longer notice. Your prospective employer will appreciate you saying that because they would like to be given the same level of courtesy and respect if they were the company losing someone.

If you are in the interview because they contacted you, either through a recruiter or some other source, just use good sense in your answer. If your employment would require a relocation, and perhaps you would need time to make arrangements, get the kids out of school, or take care of some other pressing need, just tell the truth. In my experience with hundreds of placements with dozens of corporate clients, I have found that when two parties both want the same thing to happen, they figure out a way to get it done.

I have seen situations where a job offer was made in April and the new employee had already planned a three week vacation with non-refundable deposits given, itineraries set, and the agreed start date was in mid-June. If the company wants you, and you have legitimate logistical problems, I have never seen an offer rescinded just on that basis. Sooner is generally better than later, but anything is negotiable. Companies do not want new hires starting a job when they have unresolved temporary issues weighing heavily on them. Take the time you need to get your business taken care of so that when you do start, you are fully on board mentally as well as physically.

Chapter 7

What Should You Ask Them?

Remember that a job interview is a two-way encounter. You are interviewing the company every bit as much as the company is interviewing you. Neither you nor the company is going to be better off by your working there if you are not sold on the idea that the job and the company are a good fit for your skills, experience, and expectations.

There are three main areas that you should focus on with your questions. These are the job itself, the condition of the company, and the culture of the company. Do not be hesitant about asking these questions. You are considering a major change in your life that may involve leaving your current employment, relocating, a possible loss of benefits from your current employer, and learning not only a new job, but adapting to a completely new work culture. Not only will having some good questions ready for the interviewer be helpful to you, it will be detrimental to your interests if you do not have these questions ready. Two benefits will accrue to you from having these questions ready and asking them. The first is that you will appear as prepared to the interviewer, and that is always good. The second is that you will get valuable information from the interviewer that will help you decide if it is a good match between you and the organization.

The questions you should ask depend on the position of the person who is conducting the interview. It is not uncommon for the interview process to have three or more steps. Those often include the company recruiter/HR representative, the hiring manager, and a peer or two who is doing the same type of job that you are considering. In smaller companies there may be fewer steps in the process, and one person may wear multiple hats in the organization. In that case, you can ask different types of questions to the same person. You should be aware that you will be evaluated every bit as much by the quality of the questions you ask them as you are by the answers you provide to the questions they ask you.

I lost a lot of placement fees early in my recruiting career because I spent so much time preparing candidates to answer the questions they would be asked in the interview, and not much time at all helping them craft questions that they should ask. One of the reasons I lost those placements was because I already knew the answers to most of the questions that the interviewer would normally ask during the interview and I would tell the candidates everything I knew about the company. Good recruiters know their clients very well, and generally know the answers that the corporate clients would give in response to questions the candidate might ask. However, I was missing the whole point of the process, which is so glaringly evident now that I cannot believe I did not think of it then. That point is this: Ask the questions even if you know the answers...and ask some of the same questions to everyone you meet in the interview process. Even if you already know the answers, the interviewer does not know that you know those answers. The interviewer needs to hear you ask the questions! Each person you talk to is going to be asked their impressions of you after the interview. If you get the answers from one person and then do not ask them again when you meet someone else, that next person does not know that you already asked those questions. When everyone gets together to discuss their thoughts on you, you are not going to get a good evaluation from the people to whom you did not ask good questions. If you do not ask those questions, the interviewer will likely think that either you are not very interested, or that you are not very proactive, and either one is a big negative in your chances of getting the job. Another reason to ask questions of everyone you meet is that each person will probably have different answers to the same question. The more answers and perspectives you get, the more you are going to know about the company, and the better basis you will have for making an informed decision about the organization.

In most cases, especially for larger companies, your first contact with the organization will be through the Human Resources department. The person you meet in this interview will not be the person you will report to if you get the job, but the HR representative will, in most cases, determine whether you ever meet the hiring manager. The HR rep is generally the person who writes the job description and knows not only the technical qualifications that the company is looking for, but also the type of person who will be a good match for the company's needs. He or she is a great source of information for you to learn about the company, its products and/or services, and what they are looking for in filling the position. If you do not do well in this interview, there will not be a next one. This is often called a "screening" interview.

There is a good chance, especially if you are not in the same city, that this interview will be conducted by phone rather than in-person. If that is the case, I strongly suggest that you do everything you can to be on a land line rather than a cell phone. As great as they are for our every-day communications, cell phones are still notoriously bad about dropping calls...often at the worst possible times. Also, the sound quality in most cases is not as good as what a land line provides. These screening interviews can go on for an hour or more, and the last thing you want is to tell the interviewer is that your battery is fading and that you have to stop, or worse, that the call just drops altogether. A dropped call can mean a lost opportunity. If you have no choice but to be on a cell phone, at least be in one place. Do not try to go through an interview while you are driving. Your focus should be on the road, and if it is, it is not completely on the interview. You will not be at your best, and there is a good chance that you are going to go in and out of "dead" zones where you lose reception altogether. You want to be on your game for this interview, without distractions and the sounds of traffic, sirens, road noise, or compromised driving skills detracting from your performance.

Your objective in this interview is to secure the next interview, which will most likely be with the person that you would work for and report to if you get the job. That person will also be the one who has the authority to hire you. The official offer will come from the HR department, but only with the authorization of the hiring manager. The type of questions you should ask in the HR interview should focus on the details of the job and what it is like to work for the company. The typical questions you will ask include:

1. *What can you tell me about the job?*

    You want to know not only what the job is called, but what you would actually be doing if you get it.

2. *Why is this job open right now?*

    Is it because the company is growing and it is a new position, or is it because someone else had the job and is no longer there? If that is the case, why did the previous person leave? Was this person terminated, or did he or she leave on their own accord?

3. *What can you tell me about the company culture?*

    Is it a casual atmosphere, or pretty much a high intensity work environment? What is the dress code here? Is it casual, business casual, or professional all the time? What about the inter-company protocol for communications? Is everyone on a first-name basis? Asking about the company culture is really asking the question, "How do you do things around here?" You want to get a feel for how people relate to each other as well as to customers, vendors, and the community.

4. *What is this company's mission?*

    You would be surprised at how many times this question makes people look at you with a confused stare on their faces. Asking about the company's mission is asking, "Why are you here? Why does this organizations exist?" If you cannot get a clear answer on this question, get your radar up. The better organizations will have a simple, one or two sentence mission statement that defines why they exist and what their purpose is in the industry and in the world around them. The HR rep should know what that mission is.

5.   *What can you tell me about the CEO?*

Most companies reflect the values and the attitude of the chief executive officer. No one is going to come out and say, "Our CEO is a jerk, but do not worry...you will not be working for him/her." But you will be able to tell if the HR person is genuine in what he or she tells you about the CEO. If you do not get a sincere, positive description of the CEO, again get your radar out. This does not mean that the HR person is going to give you a ten minute soliloquy about the virtues of the person at the top, but you should get a favorable, professional reply.

6.   *What type of training is provided for this position?*

Is it a formal training program in which they are going to send you off to school or an in-house training program? Will you simply be assigned to someone else who is already doing the same job so you can learn from that person? Maybe your new supervisor would be the one to teach you what they want you to know. Or, is it a "sink or swim" situation where they give you a pencil and a notepad and tell you to figure it out yourself and to get to work?

7.   *Can you give me a SWOT analysis of this company?*

In business terminology, a SWOT analysis is an examination of the Strengths, Weaknesses, Opportunities, and Threats pertaining to the company. A competent HR person should be able to give you an objective, revealing answer to that question. This is also a question that you should ask of anyone else who interviews you in the company. Each of them may have a different answer, depending on their own perspective within the company.

8.   *Can you describe the typical interview protocol for me for someone who goes forward in the process?*

You are asking how many interviews are typical in hiring someone for this position, and who else is involved.

9. *Based on what I already knew about the company and what I have learned from you today, I am very interested in moving forward in the interview process. I think it may be a great match between what the company needs and what I can bring to the job. What can I do to take the next step?*

You are saying that you are interested and that you want the job, and every company wants to hire someone who wants to be there. In just about any type of economy, and especially in a buyer's market, it is imperative that you let the interviewer know that you want the job, assuming that is, that you do want it. If you do not indicate that you want the job, your chances of going forward are reduced significantly.

10. *I appreciate your time meeting with me today. Is there anything else you need to know about me or my qualifications for this position?*

If you have done a good job before you ask this question, the answer you will probably get is that the interviewer is satisfied with what he or she has learned and you will be thanked for coming in for the interview.

11. *When can I expect to hear from you about next steps in the interview process?*

You may not get a specific answer, but you should get at least a general reply, such as "within the next week." The better employers will always let you know something one way or the other within a reasonable amount of time (one to two weeks). Asking the question and getting some kind or reply will remind them that they owe you the courtesy and respect of an answer.

There are two other questions that some job counselors recommend that you ask:

1. *How soon do you intend to fill this position?*

To me, this question makes you look a little bit foolish. The answer is almost always going to be, "When we find the right person", and they cannot really put a specific date on it. Occasionally companies will conduct preliminary interviews for positions that they intend to add at a specific date in the future, such as when an acquisition is completed or an expansion is finished. They should tell you that ahead of time

2. *How do I compare to others you are considering for this position?*

    I advise against asking this question because you are not going to get an honest answer and it makes you look stupid. No one is going to say to you, "You are the best we have seen so far." They are not going to show all their cards if there is no benefit to doing so. It also makes you appear too eager. They are also not going to say to you "Four others I have talked to look a lot better than you do." Just do your best in the interview and you should hear something one way or the other in due time.

    Assuming that you do well in the screening interview with the HR department, your next interview will typically be with the manager who can hire you and to whom you will report if you get the job. Your objective in this interview is to learn what he or she is looking for and to determine if you want to work for this person. The questions that you should ask in this interview will give you not only the information you want to know about the job, but also some keen insight into the personality and attitudes of the manager:

1. *Can you give me a description of the company's culture?*

    Yes, you have already asked this question in the interview with the HR person, but each person you ask is going to answer from a different perspective within the company. The more of those perspectives you get, the more information you will have for making a good decision about whether you want to work there.

2. *Why do customers/clients do business with this company instead of one of your competitors?*

    No matter whether you are discussing a job in sales, accounting, information technology, manufacturing, or any other department within the organization, the manager of that area is going to have a perspective on what is good about the company in the marketplace. You want to know what that is, what can be done to improve it, and whether your prospective boss is clued in on what is happening in the organization.

3.   *What skills and attributes do you think are essential for a person to do well in this job?*

The answer you get will tell you a lot about whether you are going to be successful in this job. If one of the essential elements that the manager wants and sees as necessary for success in the job is something that you do not have, the job may not be a good fit for you. Some companies and managers are very "process" oriented. They want things done a certain way, and there is very little "wiggle" room in how you do them. Other companies, however, are much more "results" oriented. They may give you a lot of flexibility in getting the job done, but they expect results. You need to know going in which way it is in this company. Understand that some companies are at the extreme one way or the other, while others operate with blend of both and fit in the middle.

4.   *Can you give me a brief SWOT analysis of this company?*

Here is another one that you have already asked the HR representative, but you want to see what kind of answer you get from the hiring manager. He or she is going to see the company from a completely different perspective than the HR person, and you want to see what is similar and what is different about their two answers.

5.   *If this is a new position, what made you decide to create it? If it is not a new position, why is it open?*

You should already know from talking to the HR person whether the position is new or not, so ask whichever question applies, but not both.

6.   *Where did you start when you joined this company, and what do you like about working here?*

The answers you get to these two questions will tell you a lot about the company and whether you want to work there. You will learn whether the company tries to promote from within or whether seeking good people from outside the organization is most common. The answer you get from the question about why he or she likes working for the company will give you a lot of insight into the personality of your prospective boss.

7. *What can you tell me about the daily or weekly routine for the person who has this job?*

You will learn whether you will be working mostly solo or with others, whether you have a lot of meetings to attend, and how much time you can expect to spend on the job. I have had clients who described jobs within the framework of an eight hour per day, five day per week routine. However, the reality was that everyone showed up at work by 6:30 or 7:00 AM, worked twelve hour days, and half a day on Saturdays. These are details that you want to know before you decide to work for the organization.

8. *Are there any unusual or unique challenges about this job that are not included in the written job description?*

This is where you will have a good shot at learning about any unusual or unique personalities within the company. If some of what you would be doing involves customers or colleagues who are, shall we say, a bit strange, this is where you will hear about it. Every company has them. Whether they choose to tell you about them is up to them, but it does not hurt to ask.

9. *What can you tell me about the company's plans for growth or expansion, either internally or through acquisitions?*

You are not going to get a specific answer if a merger or an acquisitions is in process, but you might get a general reply that says that they are always interested in growth opportunities. If they are planning on growth, you want to know as much as you can about it because that growth can either eliminate your job (if they acquire another company and get duplicate talent with it) or it could offer growth opportunities for you if they have to open new branches or expand the department.

10. *Based on what I already knew about the company and what I have learned from you today, I am very interested in moving forward in the interview process. I think it may be a great match between what the company needs and what I can bring to the job. What can I do to take the next step?*

Yes, you have already asked this question in the first interview with the HR person. Ask it again! It is especially important that you ask it if you forgot to ask it in the screening interview and were fortunate enough to move to the second interview anyway. The hiring manager wants and needs to fill this position. He or she already has a full-time job managing their part of the business. Interviewing candidates, while necessary, is a big pain for them. They want to hire someone, but they want to hire the right person. You will enhance your chances of being seen as the right person if you let them know that you want to work there and tell them why you are the right person. Asking this question may prompt a reply from the interviewer something like, "Well, tell me why you are the person we should hire!" You have to be ready if it happens. Focus on your skills that fit the job, any relevant experience, why you think you will fit well within the company culture, your work ethic, and your desire to work for the company. If you mean it when you say it, that will come across in your conversation.

11. *I appreciate your time in meeting with me today. Is there anything else you need to know about me or my qualifications for this position?*

I know, you have already asked this question in the first interview. Ask it again.

12. *When can I expect to hear from you about your decision?*

You may get an answer such as, "I will think about it and talk to the others you have met, and get back to you within a few days." You may also have done such great job that you could hear, "I'd like to set you up for a visit with our CEO (or a peer who does the same job that you would do)". Just ask the question. They owe you the courtesy of letting you know where you stand. It make take a few days, but you should expect to hear from them, either directly or from the recruiter who set you up with them (if you went through a recruiter). By your asking the question and them giving you a reply, they have a gentle reminder that they are obligated to get back to you. You may be thinking, "Well, of course they will get back to me and let me know something!" It would be nice if that were true, but I have dealt with my share of hiring authorities who either had incredibly poor memories or just felt no obligation to let people know where they stood after an interview. It is a poor reflection on a company when it happens, but it does happen occasionally.

Candidates must keep in mind that hiring managers have full time jobs of running their piece of the company, and that interviewing and communicating with candidates, while important and necessary, is not part of their regular routine. It is easy for other, more urgent (not necessarily more important) issues to take precedence over communicating with candidates.

More and more often, and because companies want to do everything they can to ensure that they make a good choice when hiring someone, they will ask you to meet with someone else who is already doing the same job that you will do if you are hired. Not only does this give them an extra voice to consider when making the hiring decision, it also gives you another perspective to consider when deciding if the job is the right one for you.

I have seen a lot of good candidates get to this stage and think that they have clear sailing toward an offer of employment. Certainly it is a good sign if the hiring manager wants you to take this step, but do not assume that it is a done deal at this point. The biggest mistake that candidates make is getting too "cozy" with the person they are asked to meet. Quite often the candidate feels that he or she can relax a little and perhaps voice an opinion or ask a question that they would not ask directly to the hiring manager or the HR representative. Be careful here. Remember that the person you are talking to has his or her first obligation to the company, not to you. Keep your questions centered on the job. If you have reservations about your prospective boss, chances are that those same reservations are apparent to the employee you are spending time with in the interview, and they will probably come out in the conversation. Your questions to the prospective peer may include these:

1. *Can you give me a description of your typical workday?*

    The answer will give you some idea of how to prioritize your activities and how you will spend your time. It will also give you some insight into the culture of the organization. Some are much more structured than others, with specific assigned activities for each day, while others are just results oriented and let you figure out how to get them.

2. *Do you like working here? Why or why not?*

    Chances are that they are not going to set you up to meet someone who is discontented with the company, so the most likely response you will get is a positive one. However, even happy employees generally have something that they do not like about the organization or the job. Be suspicious if you do not hear any reservations whatsoever, but do not be alarmed if the person you are meeting does not think the organization is perfect. Every job, and every company, has warts. Some issues that are major to one person may not be a problem at all to someone else.

3. *What do you like and/or dislike about working for your manager?*

    This is not casting stones at anyone. You are just asking for an opinion of what this person likes and does not like about his or her working relationship with the boss. Again, remember that they are not going to set you up with someone that they think is going to bash the boss or the company. Some people may see a boss who is heavily involved in their day-to-day activities as meddlesome and intrusive, while others may see the same behavior as supportive and helpful.

4. *Tell me about the training the company offers to do this job.*

    You want to know if the training is on-the-job, or do you need to go to a school or seminar somewhere to learn how to do the job. Some of the type and amount of training you will need will depend on whether you are coming from a job that was similar to this one. The answer you get will give you quite a bit of information about how the organization supports its people.

5. *Is there anything you know now that you wish you had known before you started this job?*

This is sort of a "catch-all" question. You are probably going to get information you did not know about the organization, the boss, the training, the strengths and weaknesses of the company, and anything else that the employee can bring to mind.

At the end of the meeting, thank the person for the time spent with you and if you are interested in the job, say so. Get a business card, and ask if it is OK to call if you think of any other questions. The better the impression you leave, the better report they are going to give to the hiring manager on your behalf.

There is one last matter to address at this point. What if you do not hear from them when they said they would let you know something? What if they told you they would contact you by a certain date, and that date passes without a word from them? Call them. Call the manager who told you that you would hear something. If you get that person on the phone (maybe, maybe not), extend a friendly greeting and simply say that you are still very interested in the position and have not heard anything from anyone yet. Then ask the manager if he or she can give you a status update on your candidacy for the position. Do not be concerned about coming across as impatient or worried. They told you that you would hear something, and it did not happen. There may be some very good reasons why it did not happen. Managers are generally pretty busy running their businesses, and unexpected interruptions happen all the time. Maybe time got away from them and they just forgot. It happens. Whatever the reason, you will not hurt your chances of getting the job by letting them know that you are interested in it and that you are proactive enough to pursue it.

If you do not get the manager on the phone, leave a message expressing your interest and ask for a call back. If you have not heard anything by the next day, send an e-mail to the same effect.

Chapter 8

Negotiating Your Compensation Package

The interviews have gone well. You like them. They like you. Both parties think that there is a good match and want to make this a permanent relationship. Everything seems rosy. However, there is one little detail left to consider before you can make this arrangement official. You and they need to come to an agreement on your compensation package. Your salary, bonuses, commissions, benefits, and start date have to be nailed down before you can shake hands and say, "It is a deal!"

This is the part of the job hunting process that a majority of candidates see as the most uncomfortable and anxiety-producing component in the whole experience. It does not have to be that way, and it will not be if you go into it with a good understanding of not only what you want and expect, but also what the company is trying to accomplish.

It helps to understand the organization's perspective. They have an obligation to be responsible with their money, but it has to be balanced against getting the right people for the jobs they need to fill. Good people do not leave good jobs to move sideways financially unless there are some other, very compelling reasons to do so. Even if those reasons exist, a person who feels underpaid or under-valued will stay in the new job only as long as it takes to find another one where they feel that they are closer to their real value. While the organization is not looking to be careless in how they compensate their employees, the last thing they want is to hire someone who is still looking for a job on the first day they start with the company. They want the person they hire to come to work with enthusiasm and commitment, along with plans to be there for a long time. They certainly do not want to go through the searching, interviewing, and hiring process again. Not only is the money spent in training and compensating a new hire lost when the new hire abruptly leaves the company also incurs the opportunity cost of not having someone in the position and doing the work that needs to be done.

Given all those factors, most of the companies I have dealt with in my recruiting experience have had a reasonably good handle on the market value for a given position within their organization. Compensation for similar positions varies depending on the part of the country where the job is located. Typically, the Northeast and the West Coast areas of the US have higher initial pay packages than the rest of the country. The cost of housing and many other living expenses is usually significantly higher in those areas, and companies know that they have to offer competitive compensation packages in order to attract the best people.

The best tool you can have in your favor prior to entering the negotiation phase of the process is up-to-date, valid information. Do your homework. You can get a pretty good estimate of what a given position is worth by going to www.salary.com. This website does a good job of providing ballpark salary information for most jobs, broken down by the level of experience you bring to the job and where you live. You should also do all the other research you can prior to negotiating your compensation. Before you even apply for the job, you should have some kind of idea what kind of compensation is typical for the position. Talk to others who may have had similar positions. It is critical that you have good, up-to-date information on value for the position you are seeking because once you have agreed to terms with your new employer and said "Yes" to their offer, your negotiating days are done.

Many times, if the position is advertised, there will be a range stated in the advertisement that will give you an idea what to expect. However, do not get too hung up on just the salary. More and more jobs these days have incentive packages built into the total compensation plan. A common term you will hear is "KPI", which stands for "key performance indicators". It is a common practice for organizations to offer a salary and a bonus based on achieving KPI. The amount you can earn from achieving KPI targets will vary, but the total amount will generally be a percentage of your salary. For example, if you negotiate a salary of $80,000 and the job also includes a bonus based on KPI targets, you might see a package that requires you to reach eighty percent of your KPI targets to earn any bonus. If you reach eighty percent of KPI targets, you can earn ten percent of your salary as a bonus ($8,000.00). For every five percent above eighty percent of your KPI, you can earn another five percent of your salary. So, if you reach ninety percent of your KPI targets, your bonus would be twenty percent of your salary ($16,000.00).

As you can see from this example, the amount of your salary plays a big role in the amount of bonus you can earn. If your bonus is going to be based on a percentage of your salary, you want that salary to be as high as possible. Another reason you want to maximize the amount of your salary is that salary increases are generally given as a percentage of what you are already earning. If you earn a three percent salary increase, you want that three percent to be based on a large number. As long as you stay in a particular job, your starting salary will be a big component of future earnings, both from a bonus perspective and from a salary increase perspective.

During lean times, and sometimes even in good times, some organizations try to keep from giving salary increases and instead offer bonuses as a percentage of salary. For example, if you are earning $60,000 and your employer tells everyone that due to the lean times, they are not going to give raises but instead are going to award everyone a three percent bonus, you may say, "So what...three percent is still three percent." That is true, but if and when raises start again, they will be based on the same salary you had in the for the period in which there were no raises. If your salary stays at $60,000 for two or three years, when raises come around again they will be based on that $60,000 figure. If you had received three percent raises for three years, your increase would have been based on a number that had increased three percent per year ($65,563.62) rather than on the original $60,000. Obviously, three percent of a larger number is more than three percent of a smaller number.

My point is that where you start matters. It is not the only factor that matters, but it is a big one. So, your job is to negotiate the best deal you can within the boundaries of what is typical for the position. However, what is "typical" for the position may include some other very attractive features that can, to a certain degree, offset what you may perceive as a lower than ideal salary. In many positions there are non-cash benefits ("perks") that are every bit as valuable as money in your pocket. If the compensation package that you employer offers has non-cash benefits that provide you with tools and assets that you are currently paying for out of your pocket, that is every bit as valuable (sometimes more valuable) than a comparable amount of cash compensation. For example, if you are paying for your car, gas, all maintenance and insurance on it, your computer, internet access, cell phone, monthly service fees, and you have no 401k retirement account, you are laying out a tidy sum of cash every month. If your employer offers you a car, covers all the expenses associated with it, allows personal use, gives you a cell phone and a laptop and pays for the monthly subscription plans on both, and contributes fifty cents for every dollar you put into a 401k retirement account up to six percent of your salary, that is a significant amount of money. Just the car with all the related expenses is worth at least fifteen thousand dollars a year. You will pay taxes on the benefit you receive from the car, but they pale in comparison to the taxes you would pay on the same amount of cash compensation.

The point here? Look at everything before you get too focused on just the salary.

Still, you need to be ready to sit down and negotiate the package. Here are some guidelines to help you do it most effectively:

1. *You should know before you get started whether the position you are seeking has a "fixed" compensation package or if it is negotiable.* Some sales jobs are 100% commission, and there is no salary involved. Others may have a policy where everyone starts at the same salary and any extra earnings come from commissions. Most jobs however, whether they are in sales or other fields, are not fixed in their compensation. Your experience, unique skills, and how easy it is to replace you all factor into whether you have any negotiation leverage. There are a lot of jobs that have great value, but very little negotiation leverage. Teachers have great value, but very little negotiation leverage. That is

because there are more of them out there than positions available. The employer in this case, the schools, have the upper hand in any salary negotiation. If a teacher leaves a position, the school can always find someone else to fill the position. The more unique you are and the harder it is for the employer to find someone equal to or better than you at doing the job, the more leverage you have.

While every situation is unique, it is rare that an entry level position for any kind of job is going to have much, if any, negotiation leverage. The more experience you have and the more finely tuned your skills are, the greater negotiation power you have.

2. *Do not let your thinking or your words focus on what you need.* Your needs are not their concern. The organization is going to pay what they perceive is the value of the job, and no more than that. When you think in terms of needs rather than your value, you put yourself in a weak position.

3. *Do not do any of the negotiation by mail, e-mail, or any other written communication.* Everything in the negotiation should be done in person, or at worst, by phone. You need to hear what they say and how they say it in order to react properly to their proposal. You also need the other party to see and hear you when you are presenting your position. An in-person exchange is best because there is no substitute for good, confident eye contact with the other party in negotiations. That is not possible by e-mail or by phone. The eye contact is critical. It is a great asset if used properly and a detriment if you fail at it. If you present your proposal but you are looking around the room instead of at the other party, you give the distinct impression that you do not believe in what you are saying, and your chances of success diminish considerably. The final agreement can be put into writing, and should be, but the negotiations are best done in person and in "real" time.

4. *Be the first to present a number.* It is very common for the company representative to ask something like "What are your salary requirements?", and when they do, you should be ready to give them a number. Being the first one to present a number puts you in the

position of creating an anchoring effect. That is the point at which the negotiation really starts. You want to be in the position of having them react to you rather than you reacting to them. It is like having serve position in a tennis match. You know where you are going to hit the ball and how hard you are going to hit it. The other side has to react to you and you can position yourself for the next volley when you see where they are headed to return your serve.

5. *Be ambitious!* You can lose credibility by not being aggressive enough! Studies have shown that people are happier paying more and then seeing you concede a little than they are paying less and not seeing any concessions on your part. By being aggressive at the beginning, you leave yourself room to concede. When others see you concede, they perceive that they are winning in the negotiation. One of the most common mistakes people make in negotiations is to put themselves in the other person's situation, see the rationale of their thinking, and then allow that thinking to cause them to reduce their offering before the other party asks for the concession. The key to remember is that you do not get any credit at all for concessions you make before the other side asks for them! If you allow yourself to reduce your expectations in your mind and then throw out a lower number than you otherwise would have given, you have reduced your negotiation leverage. Again, you do not benefit from any concessions that you offer before the other side asks for them. When you state an aggressive number to start the process and thereby set the anchor point, the other side is already in a position of conceding something to you. They want to see you concede something as well. They cannot see it if you do it in your head before you speak.

If you decide before you present a number to the other party that you are going to lower that number, they do not know that you originally had a higher number in mind. The other party needs to see and *hear your* concession. It is part of the negotiating protocol that each side "keeps score" on concessions made. Neither party wants to be the one that makes all the concessions. Even though you may think to yourself that you have conceded on a particular point, if the other side does not see and hear it, you do not get credit for it.

Another reason that you want to be the first one to say a number is to avoid the "winners curse." We have all had experience with it, but not everyone knows what it is called. Assume for a moment that you are selling a car and that you want to sell the car for two thousand dollars. You have placed an ad in the paper, and someone shows up to look at it. They ask you what you want for it, and you reply, "Two thousand dollars." The buyer responds by immediately saying, "You have got a deal...gimme the keys...gimme, gimme, gimme..."

You are a little taken aback. You expected to bargain a little and that you might even have to lower your price to sell the car, but now the buyer eagerly makes the deal and is gleefully ready to drive off in his car. What are you thinking? You are thinking that you did not ask nearly enough for the car and that you could have sold it for considerably more than two thousand dollars. The same thing can happen in salary negotiations, and it will eat at you every day that you show up for work if you have the feeling that you left money on the table.

Hiring authorities know and understand that an increase in compensation is a prime motivator for making a job change. They do not expect you to move sideways (stay the same). They know that you expect to do better in the new position than you would by staying where you are, and that they have to make the move attractive in order to get you to make it. You have no reason to seek only a modest "bump" in compensation, so do not hesitate to seek your value. The other party is not going to be offended or insulted by you seeking what you think you are worth. By the time you get into compensation negotiations, they have already decided that you are the one, or one of a very few candidates that they want to hire for this position. All that is left to do is set the price.

6.   *Avoid speaking in ranges.* Give specific figures. If you say, "I was thinking of something in the range of ninety to one hundred thousand dollars", the only thing the other side hears is "ninety

thousand dollars." They have absolutely no incentive to give you one penny more than that because you have already told them that it is an acceptable figure. Nothing that you say after that is going to make any difference, even if you mutter something about how the amount you would expect would depend on the responsibilities of the job. Everything you say after you mention the lower figure is irrelevant, so do not say it. State an ambitious figure, not a range. If the other party is unwilling or unable to go there, they will tell you, but you will arrive at a better figure if you set a high point and then concede than if they set a low one and you try to increase it.

7. *Know your BATNA, and consider theirs.* The acronym "BATNA" stands for "best alternative to a negotiated agreement." It is what you have as a fallback position if you are unable to come to an agreement. If the two parties cannot come to an agreement, your BATNA is your state of affairs that you go back to in lieu of starting the new job. If you know what yours is and you know how much better things will have to be in order for you to consider leaving it, you have the basis for how to decide "yes" or "no" to the new opportunity.

There is no "one size fits all" figure for how much a new opportunity has to pay in order to justify leaving your present position. However, if you are happy where you are and there are no other compelling reasons to make the move (such as better location, more opportunity for advancement, or job satisfaction) a good rule of thumb is that a new opportunity ought to give you at least a fifteen percent pay increase in order to justify the change. Changing jobs, for all the good things it can represent, can also be a major life disruption. It is a lot easier to accept and justify those disruptions if you can say to yourself that you are being compensated for them.

The status quo (your present circumstances) is always a "sticky" situation, meaning that we are reluctant to change it unless there is a (or several) really good reason to do so. If you go into a negotiation knowing what your current BATNA is and you have decided that it will take a fifteen percent improvement to justify changing it, you are well armed for objective and constructive negotiation. The key is to decide what that number is before the negotiations start. When you decide what that number is before the negotiations begin, you do so with a clear head that is free of the pressures of the moment when you are more likely to lose some degree of objectivity.

The other side also has a BATNA. They may not know it by that name, but they have one, and you will do yourself a big favor if you consider it before the negotiations begin. If you are one of a thousand people whom they could find to do the job, their BATNA is a lot stronger than yours, and you should plan on using your finely honed negotiating skills in future opportunities after you have gained a little experience. In this initial position, you are not in much of a position to bargain. However, if you have been around for a while and have gained considerable expertise in your field...if you have some "skins on the wall"...you have some bargaining power. Part of that bargaining power comes from the fact that if the company is in compensation negotiations with you, there is something about you that they want more than the others they have considered for this position. Some of the elements of their BATNA may include:

1. That someone else will have to "double up" and do their job and this one until they can find someone to fill it, and that neither job will be done as well as if there was someone in each position.

2. That they will have to continue the search, taking time away from other, more pressing responsibilities until they find the right person.

3. That you were the one that they chose to fill the position, so there must be some good reasons why they want you from among all the others they considered.

4. That the opportunity cost of not having someone in the position and doing the job is substantial, and that failing to come to an agreement with you extends and continues those costs.

Remember during the entire process that you are negotiating the *entire* compensation package, not just the salary. If the salary you mention is $100,000, and they say "Great, it's a deal" but they do not offer you a car (or whatever else you value as part of the package you seek), you will end up worse off than if they offered you $90,000 and included a car in the package. Do not simply assume that anything specific is included in your package. You have to be sure that you and the other side are clear about the whole package, not just individual parts of it.

There can be any number of reasons why they chose you instead of someone else. They key is to remember that they are trying to hire you. They are not trying to avoid hiring you. It is been my experience in hundreds of negotiations that when both parties want the same result to occur, they find a way to get it done.

Chapter 9

How to Resign from a Job

Accepting a new job brings all kinds of changes to your life...new opportunities, new routines, new environments, and new relationships. However, before any of the "new" can begin, you have to get out of the "old". You will need to resign from the job that you already have in order to take the new one, and resigning is not as easy or as simple as you might think.

Depending on the reasons that you have accepted a new job, resigning from the old one is often an uncomfortable, but necessary task. Maybe you loved the job and the people you worked with, but the new job offered opportunities that you just could not pass up. Perhaps you have been looking for a new job for a long time because you cannot stand the job that you have or the people you work with. Either way, there is a right way and a wrong way to make your exit, and it is to your benefit (both immediate and long term) to do it the right way.

Your main focus in leaving the old job should be to do it in such a way that you do not leave on bad terms. That is not to say that your leaving might not upset someone, but there should not be any words or deeds on your part that creates unnecessary animosity or burns any bridges. You may be tempted to tell a few people what you really think of them, but resist the impulse. If you handle the resignation with professionalism and respect, you will always be better off than if you leave a sour taste in the mouths of your former associates. This is particularly true if you are staying in the same industry. Word gets around, and nothing stays a secret for very long. Your words and your deeds will follow you. Also, it is not at all uncommon for companies to merge with or acquire others in the same industry, and you may find yourself re-united with the folks that you used to work with at the "old" job.

Before you turn in your resignation, either verbally or in writing, there are a few details that you should take care of to avoid an awkward departure:

1. Be sure that any company property in your possession is with you so that you can give it back at the time you resign. If you have a laptop, get rid of any personal software and files. Give it back to them "clean." If there is any other equipment, files, supplies, etc...that you have, bring it back to its rightful owner, the company.

2. Get the details about when new benefits start at the new company that will replace those you have at the old job. Be clear about when your insurance stops at the old job and when you are eligible for benefits in the new company. In many companies there is a ninety to one hundred twenty day waiting period before you can be eligible for coverage. If that is the case, be aware of what you can do to continue the coverage you have with the old company for a time after you leave until the new coverage starts.

3. Know where you stand on any commissions, vested benefits, vacation time, sick leave, personal days, or any other compensation due to you. Some companies have policies that say you must still be employed as of a certain date to receive any compensation earned prior to that date. If your old employer has a policy manual, read it. It probably has that information in it.

4. Have any personal property, photos, certificates, books, or other personal effects collected and ready to pick up and leave with after you submit your resignation.

So, now that you have covered those details, it is time to actually tell your boss that you are leaving. Here are some guidelines on how and when to do that:

1. Schedule a time in the late afternoon to meet with your supervisor in his or her office. Go in and close the door.

2. Have your written letter of resignation prepared and signed, in an envelope, and hand it to your supervisor. Say that you are there to tender your resignation.

3. The typical departure notice has been two weeks, but some companies may ask for more in their policy handbook. A good rule of thumb is to offer the same number of weeks as you have in vacation benefits. If you get three week's vacation, offer three week's notice that you are leaving.

4. If possible, offer to help find and train your replacement. This can be an invaluable service to your employer, and will certainly help sustain a positive image of you in their eyes.

5. Continue to earn your paycheck while you are still there. Do not be a "slacker."

6. Take care to leave detailed written instructions, guidelines, passwords, keys, access codes, combinations, contact information, and any other essential information for the company to use when you are gone and someone else has to do the job you had.

7. Do not poison the environment by voicing your displeasure about anything or anyone that may have been bothering you while you were there. You will be out of there soon enough.

8. Remember the Golden Rule. Treat others like you want to be treated. Be reasonable if your boss asks you for any specific help in making the transition a smooth one.

Once you actually tell your boss that you are leaving, do not be surprised or caught off guard if one of these circumstances occur:

1. You may be asked to leave immediately, and perhaps even escorted out of the building. In some organizations, the protocol is to have someone accompany you to your desk, watch you gather your belongings, and then see you out the door. That is why you should have everything ready to go before you announce your resignation. You should know ahead of time, if this happens, whether you then have a vacation for a few weeks before you start the new job, or you can begin immediately.

2. You may become "persona non grata", which means they take it personally and you go from formerly valued and respected employee to traitorous turncoat. Do not let that dictate how you respond. Take the high road and continue to conduct yourself honorably and professionally, regardless of how they treat you.

3. Your boss and co-workers may implore you to stay and try to make you feel guilty about deserting them. Stand firm in your decision. This can be a very difficult time, and you are not going to be in your best decision-making state of mind. Do not let emotion override good sense.

4. You may receive a counter offer to stay there and turn down the new position. With very few exceptions, changing your mind and staying is not in your best interests. I have seen this happen at least a dozen times in my career of placing people in new companies. In one of those situations where the candidate changed his mind and stayed, it worked out OK and he did well, but that is more the exception than the rule. I have seen at least five instances where the candidate stayed, and in each of those instances, the company let that person go within a year. The other opportunity was gone, and the worker was unemployed for months afterward.

Ask yourself this question: If they offer you more money to stay, why weren't they paying you that amount in the first place? If you are worth it only when you say you are leaving, why were you not worth it already? Well, the real and honest answer to that question is "because they did not have to." The company does not exist for your benefit. It hires and pays people only because it gets more in return for the expenditure than it pays out, and there is nothing wrong with that state of affairs as long as you understand and realize it. By offering you a larger, better package to stay, the company is simply continuing to protect its interests. However, if you decide to stay and refocus your energies to the benefit of your old employer, whether you realize and admit it or not, you are branded. You are branded as someone who was willing to leave, and you will never shake that label. When the new opportunity is no longer there and you are back in your "old" job, you have given the hammer to your old employer. Unless you have a contract that guarantees your employment and compensation, the company can decide at any time that their interests are best served by taking the time to find your replacement and then ridding themselves of someone who was willing to leave earlier for a better opportunity.

What is the lesson? If you do decide to stay (and I advise against it very strongly), get it in writing what they are going to pay you and for how long if they let you go. Remember that you have a strong BATNA (the other offer), so you have nothing to lose by doing all you can to protect yourself from loss of income later if they change their mind about how valuable you are to them.

When you announce that you are leaving, you may be asked to meet with someone from Human Resources for an exit interview. You do not have to do it, but I would recommend that you do. Human Resources is obviously interested in why you are leaving. If there is a problem within the company, they certainly want to know about it so that they can take steps to correct it. However, just because they want to know everything (and you cannot blame them for asking) does not obligate you to tell everything. This is not the time for "paybacks". Be professional, courteous, and brief. Stay away from pettiness, vendettas, personality conflicts, and anything else that would burn a bridge. If you are leaving for a better opportunity, you can say so, but the details of your new job and your compensation are no one else's business.

Your letter of resignation should be brief and to the point. You do not have to give the reason for your decision to leave, but if you do, do not elaborate:

Dear _____

I am resigning my position as (job title), and offering two weeks notification of my departure. I have accepted another position that I believe will help me achieve some of my important career goals.

I will do all that I can to help in the smooth transition of my responsibilities to someone else before leaving.

I appreciate the time I spent at (name of the organization) and I wish you the best going forward.

Sincerely,
Your Name

Sign it and keep a copy. Do things the right way until you leave.

Chapter 10

Working with a Recruiter

There is no question that the best way to jump-start your career search is through people you know, especially if you know someone in the company where you want to work. If you are fortunate enough to be in that situation, take advantage of it. However, if you do not have that luxury you have to go about your search in other ways.

Companies use outside recruiters for a variety of reasons, but probably the most common of those reasons is that good recruiters save companies a lot of time, and saving time is saving money. Most recruiters focus on industries where they had personal experience working themselves. They know the key players in industry, they speak the vocabulary, and they know how the industry operates.

Most companies have limited exposure to people who do not work for that company or who are not either customers of or suppliers to that company. Because of that limited exposure, companies themselves do not have the immediate knowledge of where to go to find the best people to fill a particular position. That is why they call an outside recruiter. It saves them time and allows them to continue doing the real work in their organizations while the recruiter is engaged in the searching for people and the mind-numbing resume evaluations that are part of any successful search and placement.

There is a very good chance that at some point in your career you will be contacted by a recruiter who is representing a client company and is engaged in finding the right person for a particular position within that company. If you have not been contacted by one, you may be interested in making the contact yourself with the recruiter if you are interested in making a job change. Whether you are contacted by the recruiter or the recruiter contacts you, there are a few guidelines that help you get the most benefit out of the association.

The first and most important point for you to understand is that the recruiter's fee is paid by the client company. It should not cost you any money at all to deal with any recruiter. If you are told by a recruiter that he or she can find you a job if you pay a fee for their services, hold onto your wallet and exit the relationship as fast as possible. Because the fees are paid by the companies and not the candidates, the recruiter's first loyalty is going to be toward the company. The recruiter's job is to find high quality candidates that fit the criteria that the client company has provided. In short, their job is to find people for jobs, not to find jobs for people.

Candidates do not often understand this relationship. They may send a recruiter a resume, and then when they have not heard anything back for a few days, start to wonder why the recruiter has not called with some job interview schedules. It does not work like that. Most recruiters are inundated with unsolicited resumes every week. Forty to fifty unsolicited resumes per week is pretty standard in my own business, but unless I have an active search that is a good fit for one of them, it is very unlikely that the person who sent it to me will receive a response.

If you are contacted by a recruiter and you are told about a job that interests you, there are a few guidelines you can follow to maximize your chances of getting the results you want from the association:

1. *Do not ask who the company is that the recruiter is representing.* One of the reasons that the company is using the recruiter in the first place is to put a buffer between themselves and all the candidates who are not a good fit for the job. It is the recruiter's job to do the sifting and the sorting, and then present to the company the best of the candidates they have found in the search. It is a very time-consuming and tedious process. The company does not want to hear directly from the candidates themselves at this stage of the search because they do not want to take the time to do the sifting and sorting. If after talking to you and evaluating whether you are a good

fit for the job, the recruiter decides that you are indeed someone worth presenting to the company, the recruiter will give you the information you need in order to prepare for the first contact with the company.

2. *Tell the truth.* Do not represent yourself as something you are not. Do not claim degrees that you do not have, and do not try to hide potential black marks on your job history or your personal history. Those things are going to come out sooner or later anyway in background checks. Recruiters cannot make any money until they place someone in a job, so if you are qualified, they are going to do everything they can to help you succeed. If you have some issues that may not be very pretty in your past, the recruiter can often intercede for you in such a way that the issues you saw as obstacles may not be as big as you think. But they cannot do anything for you if you are not open and honest about the information they need to know.

3. *Understand that nothing in the hiring process happens as fast as you think it should.* Once again, you and the recruiter have the same priority. You both want things to move faster than they do. You cannot start work until you are hired, and the recruiter cannot send an invoice to the client until you start working. However, the client companies also have a business to run while they are trying to fill the position. It may be the most urgent and important issue going on with you at the time, but it certainly is not the top or only priority for the client company. They set the pace, and they control the flow of events. Get used to it.

4. *Be available.* That does not mean that you have to sit by the phone all day every day in case the recruiter calls. It does however, mean that if the recruiter is trying to reach you, you should not be hard to find. Call back if you get a message asking you to do so. Check your e-mail regularly. If you are asked to provide information in a timely manner, do it. One key quality that recruiters and hiring managers both like to see in candidates is a sense of responsibility and urgency. If you take a day or two to call back or reply to an e-mail, you are giving an indication to the recruiter that you will probably

act the same way on the job. If the recruiter begins to sense that you are not as committed as they are toward getting you an interview and possibly a job offer, they will cease their efforts to help you and drop you as a candidate. They are judged by their client companies on the basis of the quality of the candidates they submit to the company. They are not going to send someone in to represent them before the client if they sense that you are not going to put them in a favorable light.

5.   *Listen to what the recruiter tells you.* You and the recruiter have a common goal, which is to get you hired. You both win when that happens. If the recruiter offers you suggestions on how to improve your chances for getting an interview, such as a way to improve your resume, listen to the suggestion and then do it. If you have ever sold a house through a realtor, you probably got advice from the realtor about how to "stage" your house so that it would be most attractive to potential buyers. The same thing is happening here, except you are the product being sold. The recruiter may advise you on how to dress, what to say, and what to do in your interactions with the client. The recruiter knows the client better than you do, and the company has entrusted the recruiter to act on their behalf to find people. Take advantage of that knowledge and use it to help you present yourself in the most favorable light.

6.   *Respect the recruiter's time and efforts.* If the recruiter selects you as someone they think is a good fit for the position, they going to invest considerable time and effort into helping you get the job. In order to give you their best efforts, they need your cooperation. They are not interested in, nor do they have the time for salvage projects or people who cannot seem to keep a job. Recruiters want to work with people who are responsible, enthusiastic, dependable, and who do their part to ensure a successful outcome of their mutual efforts. They are particularly interested in getting feedback from you about the interview process, the people you meet during the interviews, the questions you were asked and that you asked the company representatives. They can help you immeasurably if you keep them in the loop once the interview process starts.

Summary

There is nothing easy about finding the right job for you. Even under the best of circumstances the process can take weeks or months. It can be discouraging if you give it your best efforts without success for weeks and months on end, and it can be difficult to see how every little detail can really make a difference. In many cases it comes down to the law of numbers. The more attempts you make, the greater your chances of success. However if you can reduce that time by even a small amount by paying attention to these little details, you will find that the effort was worth it.

There is one more factor in your job search that can and will be a big influence on your success. That factor is your attitude as you proceed through the process. Nature tends to weed out the slow, the weak, and those that are not alert to their surroundings. The job market, fairly or not, can be a microcosm of the world around us. Nobody wants to hire someone who seems to be uninspired, tired, or downcast. I see it quite often in people I interview. They may have the technical skills and the experience, but when they come across as weary, dejected, or as if they expect rejection, that is pretty much what they will find. Your attitude comes across to others even if it is in a phone conversation rather than a personal interview. You have to understand that employers want to hire winners, and everything about you contributes to the impression you make on others. It is not easy to keep plowing ahead with energy, enthusiasm, and a positive outlook when the search has been difficult and unsuccessful for a while, but that is exactly what you have to do if you want to succeed in the hunt.

The reason that the strategies, suggestions, and guidelines listed in these pages are there is because they work. The more you apply them, the better you get in the performance, and the more likely you are to find success. The right job for you is out there, and with these tools you are equipped to find it and start your new career.

Special thanks to Randolph G. Bias, Ph.D. for his review and editing of this book. The book is much better than it would have been without his help.

www.ingramcontent.com/pod-product-compliance
Lightning Source LLC
Chambersburg PA
CBHW021545200526
45163CB00015B/1645